THE BEST FRIEND'S GUIDE TO BREAST CANCER

WHAT TO DO IF YOUR BOSOM BUDDY OR LOVED ONE IS DIAGNOSED

SONJA L. FAULKNER, Ph.D.

thebestfriendsguidetobreastcancer.com

811 615 694
JAN 2 5 2013 7/

For Aunt Claudette

The bravest warrior I know

Foreword

Almost inevitably, the concerned and loving friends or family members of a woman recently diagnosed with breast cancer will struggle with what to do and say. How do you encourage, support, and inspire without unwittingly offending, fatiguing, or disappointing the person you love? Whereas most breast cancer patients become consumed by their own battles, Sonja Faulkner becomes consumed by you, dear reader…

Through the wisdom of experience, Sonja and other breast cancer survivors provide honest and insightful advice about the friends they either cherished, or wished they had known. Sonja guides you through all phases of an illness from diagnosis to cure, prepares you with the breast cancer basics, creates accurate expectations about treatment, and offers practical suggestions that will make your friend's rough road a little smoother (from reassuring one-liners to recipes like "Mum's Minestrone Soup").

Foreword

As a breast cancer surgeon for over 10 years, I have treated thousands of women with breast issues, witnessing firsthand the healing power of social support. You do not need to be a breast cancer survivor to impact a woman with your positive words and thoughtful actions. If you know someone who has been diagnosed with breast cancer, <u>The Best Friend's Guide to Breast Cancer</u> will prove to be an uplifting, comprehensive resource. A must-read for friends and loved ones!

Kristi Funk, MD, FACS
Breast Cancer Surgeon
Founder and Director, Pink Lotus Breast Center
Los Angeles
October, 2011

As a practicing oncologist for the past eight years, I can attest to the importance of social support during the treatment process. This wonderful, well-written guide is all someone needs to provide the much-needed support to their friend or family member facing a breast cancer diagnosis or going through treatment.

Many books have been published to aid the individual on their journey. However, Ms. Faulkner's guide fills the previously unmet need of material to help loved ones in this process. I will recommend Sonja's book to all of my patients and their families.

Noam Drazin, MD, Hematology/Oncology

Foreword

Beverly Hills
November, 2011

Acknowledgments

To the insightful women who shared their breast cancer stories with me, thank you for your honesty and contributions to this guide. Your wisdom will help others understand the road we travel. You are all brave and beautiful warriors.

À Christian et Caden Gray, tout simplement, vous êtes ma raison d'être et je vous aime beaucoup.

To Mum, Daddy, Lorraine, Joe, and Jack, you are my rocks and soft places to land. You've lifted me up and held me close through the trying times and been an integral part of life's most joyful moments. I love you all so much.

To my medical team, I wish everyone diagnosed with breast cancer could receive the high level of care and expertise that you provided. The following individuals deserve recognition and my deepest gratitude:

Dr. Suzanne Gilberg-Lenz, my OB/GYN, who gave me two of the greatest gifts of my life: you

brought my beautiful son into the world and sent me
to Dr. Kristi Funk's Pink Lotus Breast Center, which
put me on the path to wellness. You took the time to
call on several occasions after my diagnosis to check
in. I'll always be grateful for your care and concern.
Thank you.

Dr. Kristi Funk, my breast surgeon: you guided
me and took exceptional care of me during the scariest
health crisis of my life. Your kind bedside manner
continues to comfort me, and I feel incredibly
reassured with you in my corner. You are a world-
renowned surgeon, yet I feel like I'm getting together
with a trusted girlfriend when I see you. Thank you
so much for everything.

Dr. Leif Rogers, my reconstructive surgeon:
you are a superstar, a true artist. Honestly, your talent
and expertise are unrivaled! Thank you for helping
me through what could have been a traumatizing
event with your sensitivity and grace.

Dr. Noam Drazin, my oncologist: In The
Wizard of Oz, Dorothy had her scarecrow. I have
you. Thank you for always looking out for me and
making me feel safe and secure. You were one of my
biggest supporters through chemotherapy and
beyond, and I know I wouldn't have done as well
with anyone else. Oncology offices are not always
joyful places, but I've never laughed so hard during
medical appointments. Thank you for taking such
good care of me and reminding me that there's still
plenty of room for smiles during the cancer journey.

Finally, to my incredible friends: this effort has
been a letter of love to you. You're all treasures.

Acknowledgments

Thank you!

The Purpose of This Book

There are hundreds of books for the person who has been diagnosed with cancer (many are very good, including Vicki Girard's There's No Place Like Hope, which resonated with me). But what if you're the best friend or loved one of someone who's received the news that will change her life forever? It can be a frightening and uncertain time for you, too. You may be nervous about what to say (and what not to say) and unsure how to help your friend. Regardless of where she is in her breast cancer journey, this guide will offer insight about what your friend may be thinking, suggestions for communicating with her, tips on how you can help, and gift ideas. Included are memorable quotes from other breast cancer survivors, and together, we'll coach you through each phase of your friend's illness--whether you're female or male.

When talking to your friend during the course of her diagnosis, treatment, and recovery, you'll hear an onslaught of medical information and terminology.

The Purpose of This Book

An overview of breast cancer basics, treatment options, and health maintenance is included in the guide to assist you in understanding what your friend is facing. Believe me, she'll be grateful if she doesn't have to explain every last detail of each test or procedure. Those of us battling cancer get tired, both physically and emotionally, so you—as an informed buddy—can be a genuine gift. Note that there is much to digest in the medical sections, and occasionally you may choose to skip ahead to other topics. It's easy to refer back to breast cancer basics, treatment options, and health maintenance as needed.

Food is incredibly important and deserves its own chapter. I fall into the camp that believes 1) it's medicine, and 2) it's love. To me, a nutritious and delicious meal is one of the most wonderful ways to show a friend you care. In chapter 4, I'll discuss the experts' list of super cancer-fighting foods and why they receive high marks. Also, you'll find many easy recipes in the appendix to make for your pal during every stage of her battle. Your loving preparation of food for her, particularly when she's just not up to cooking, will fill her heart as well as her tummy.

The guide also provides lists of organizations and websites where you can learn more about breast cancer, receive support, find information on events or walks, and opportunities to volunteer, make a donation, or become an advocate.

Unfortunately, this is a disease that touches everyone. According to the American Cancer Society, one in eight women will develop breast cancer in their lifetime.[1] You have a unique opportunity to be a source of strength, support, and light to a loved one who has been diagnosed. Knowing that you care will sustain and uplift her, I promise.

Keep in mind that best friends come in many forms. A best buddy can be a girlfriend, husband, sister, mother, brother, boyfriend, co-worker, or cousin. The most important criterion is the bond you share with the woman diagnosed with breast cancer. This book honors and acknowledges all of you.

As someone who has fought breast cancer and been the friend to many others diagnosed, I want to help you through this trying time. Please know that you have the power to make a significant difference in a woman's life.

Finally, thank you to all of the extraordinary best friends out there!

*Please note that the pronouns "she" and "her" are used throughout the book due to the overwhelming majority of female breast cancer cases. It is not my intention, however, to leave men out of this discussion. Unfortunately, they are diagnosed with breast cancer, too. Here are some statistics from the American Cancer Society: 2

- About 2,100 new cases of invasive breast cancer are diagnosed among men each year, with 450 men losing their battle
- Men comprise less than 1% of all breast cancer cases, and the majority of those diagnosed are between 60 and 70 years old

- A man's lifetime risk of being diagnosed with breast cancer is 1 in 1,000

In addition to the fear of a life-threatening illness, men often face unique challenges with a breast cancer diagnosis. Because it is rare, male breast cancer doesn't receive the same level of attention or awareness as female breast cancer. Also, men may feel alone in their battle and stigmatized for having a "female" disease. Traditionally, many men haven't felt comfortable expressing fear or pain; thus, there is tremendous potential for isolation after a breast cancer diagnosis.

The important point, though, is that the themes in this guide also apply to men living with breast cancer. They are universal rules of love, support, and communication. Please remember that the gamut of loss is significant for both men and women.

For male breast cancer support, www. mdjunction.com/male-breast-cancer is a "community of patients, family members, and friends dedicated to dealing with male breast cancer, together."

Table of Contents

Table of Contents

Appendices

Introduction

The most important nugget of advice I can offer is simple, and I base this on both my personal experience as well as what other breast cancer survivors shared with me about their journey. Without question, the most valuable gift you can offer is to reach out. I'd be lying if I said I wasn't disappointed in some people who disappeared during my diagnosis and treatment, including friends I had known for many years. More often, though, people showed they cared, and I was filled with gratitude each time I received an unexpected phone call, funny card, quick e-mail to check in, soulful letter, or thoughtful care package (and I don't just mean generous, I mean truly thoughtful, as in, put a lot of thought into the contents). If I was ever having a rough day, all I needed to do was replay in my head an act of kindness to get me back on the warrior path.

I know how lucky I am. For me, the outpouring of love, support, and encouragement was overwhelming, and incidentally, not just from people I knew well. Those I didn't know well or folks from the past (way, way past in some cases) blew me away with their concern and offers of help. I'll be thankful for the rest of my life for each gesture, grand or small. As I discovered, though, even small gestures become grand. The "I'm thinking of you today" email, for example, takes very little effort or time but means the world to someone fighting cancer. Which brings me back to my original point: just reach out. If you don't, we might assume that you don't care all that much, or that you don't think we're worth the bother. And what friend would want to make that mistake?

Even if your girlfriend was diagnosed some time ago and you haven't contacted her because of any number of reasons, know that it's never too late. Don't allow the fear or embarrassment you may be feeling prevent you from letting her know that she's on your mind.

Remember, this is a marathon and not a sprint. There may be a time when you trip over your words or say the wrong thing. You're only human, after all! You may feel awkward and worry that you're doing more harm than good. Perhaps your instinct will be to flee or give up, but hang in there. Be present for the long haul. Your friendship is a truly unique and beautiful gift, and the love and support you offer your pal will help her through even the darkest days.

Chapter 1

The Diagnosis

The following section is meant to give insight as to what your friend may be feeling, not offer suggestions on how to help.

What your friend may be thinking

A breast cancer diagnosis will likely knock the wind out of your friend, shaking up her world as she knows it, calling into question how the universe works, and generally leaving her with a feeling of, "holy crap." Plus, let's face it: cancer is never convenient and always a disruption, so logistically there's much to figure out.

My baby boy turned ten months-old the week I was diagnosed. I had struggled for years to have him and was enjoying motherhood—the breastfeeding, changing poopy diapers, everything—blissfully unaware that all hell was about to be unleashed. To quote Charles Dickens, it was the best of times, it was the worst of times. The darkest moments visited me when I thought about him. Sometimes I'd turn into a blubbery mess when I envisioned him growing up without me. My primary concern was for my boy, but I was serving up a big slice of selfish pie, too. I wanted to watch this delicious creature grow up and see the person he would become.

The timing of the diagnosis was terrible, but I have to admit that having a baby who depended on me helped me focus and fight to get well. If ever I needed incentive to call upon a warrior spirit, he was it.

My whip-smart OB-GYN, Dr. Suzanne Gilberg-Lenz, calls this the survivor mode kicking in, and many women I spoke to expressed that this singular focus on thrashing cancer's butt happens soon after a diagnosis. Of course, everyone's story and cancer experience is unique, but often some semblance of Elisabeth Kubler-Ross's stages of grief make an appearance during the battle: shock, denial, anger and confusion, bargaining, sadness and depression, and finally, acceptance. [3]

Shock: For many, the news of breast cancer is such a stunner that one may not fall apart right away. On paper, my doctors told me that I was the last person who should get cancer. After a couple of diagnostic procedures early on, my wonderful and caring breast surgeon, Dr. Kristi Funk, gently suggested that I have someone come with me to my next appointment. I pooh-poohed that hint and insisted on seeing her alone. As we sat there going over the diagnosis and treatment strategies, I listened intently like a dutiful student, never once getting emotional. It was as if the entire experience was happening to someone else, and I was a voyeuristic intruder. I thanked her, told her I would see her soon, and was on my way. When I got home, I found a note my husband had left on the kitchen counter saying that he was out with our son for a stroller ride in the neighborhood. I had a hunch where they might be, so I set out to find them. I spotted them in the distance coming toward me, and once close enough, my baby recognized me and started jumping up and down in his seat, flailing his arms about, and offering me the most joyful expression imaginable. He was as thrilled to see me as I was to see him. It was exactly what I needed in that moment, and it's forever etched in my memory. It made me cry, though, too. At the time, it seemed like the universe was pulling a rotten prank, giving me this beautiful baby and then making me face my mortality.

Denial: Your friend may be in denial after the initial shock wanes. For me, I asked more than once, "How could this be happening—especially now?" I was busy and didn't have time to accommodate cancer's schedule. Plus, I felt fine, had always been the picture of health, and did my best to take care of myself. I had a mental picture of a cancer patient, and she didn't look like me. Was this really happening?

Anger and Confusion: Someone diagnosed with

breast cancer is likely to have moments of confusion and feeling pissed off. Cancer is not only scary, but hugely disruptive, too. Your friend may be baffled about why this is happening to her and question what she did to deserve it. She may feel overwhelmed by all that's in front of her, including the logistics of health care expenses, work, child care, her home, relationships...the list goes on and on. She may also feel like her world has turned into one of those frightening Midwest tornadoes, spinning wildly out of her control. With a little luck, this stage won't consume her. I think having a fire in her belly is a good thing if it spurs her to action or gives her a fighting spirit. But if she lets it take over, it will wreak havoc on her mind, body, and spirit. As tempting as it might be at times, I can't think of anything good that comes from staying furious at your body, your lot in life, or the world.

Bargaining: The bargaining stage for someone diagnosed with breast cancer might go like this: "If ___, then ___." If I stop smoking, then let me live. If I promise to eat all of my vegetables each day for the rest of my life, then let me keep my breasts. If I lose weight, then let me never have to worry about cancer again. If I'm a nicer person and never say a mean thing and don't complain about anything ever, ever, ever, then just get me through this ordeal. I suppose this is our mind's attempt to regain some perceived control over our situation: I can control (fill in the blank) in the future, now you—the universe, God, whomever—just make this go away! In this stage, I promised the universe that I would be a more positive person, stop worrying about so much, and take more time to be grateful for all of the blessings in my life, if I could just be alive and well for my son.

Sadness and Depression: The spectrum for despair is wide in this stage. For some, a little self-pity for a short period of time is enough to lean into acceptance. For others, a mourning period of the previous reality, along with one's corresponding dreams and plans, must take place—grieving what coulda-shoulda-woulda been. And then there are those who get stuck in this stage and have difficulty shaking feelings of hopelessness, bitterness, and melancholy.

Acceptance: This is a wonderfully empowering stage, because the person with breast cancer isn't discounting the pain it's causing, nor the fear, disruption, or chaos; rather, she's simply saying, "Okay, I have cancer. It's part of my new reality and I'm moving on. What's next?" This is the I-don't-have-time-for-the-bullshit phase. Plans are made and strategies implemented, such as treatment options. For me, things started to get much clearer in terms of how and with whom I wanted to spend time and share experiences, short and long-term goals, all sorts of stuff. It was an unexpected gift in an otherwise uncertain time.

Breast cancer basics: Understanding the medical jargon

As fun and fabulous as breasts are, the unsexy truth is that they exist primarily to nourish a baby. On the outside, each woman's breasts are as unique as fingerprints. Inside, however, their composition is the same across the board (see Figure 1.1). Breasts are made up of:

- lobules, the grape-like sacs that make milk

- ducts, the tubes that carry milk from the lobules to the nipple

- fatty tissue, which supports the lobules and ducts

- connective tissue, which holds the breast in place

- blood vessels to transport nutrients and oxygen to the breast

- lymphatic tissue and lymph vessels, which carry potentially harmful bacteria and viruses (as well as immune cells) to filters called lymph nodes, which help the body fight infection

- a major group of muscles called pectorals that are behind the breast and attached to ribs

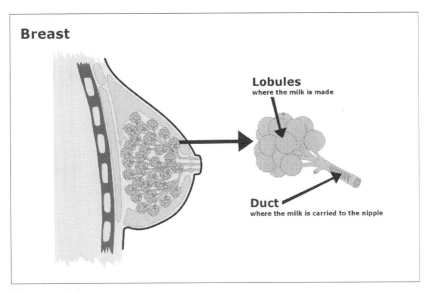

Figure 1.1

What is breast cancer?

Breast cancer is a complex topic, and heavy-duty science explanations are beyond the scope of this book. At 700+ pages, Dr. Susan Love's Breast Book can answer any question you may have about the biology of cancer.

With that said, here's a super-condensed, layperson's version of what happens when cancer invades a breast: the tissue and organs in our bodies are made of millions and millions of cells. These cells divide at a steady rate, with the new replacing the old, so that each organ functions normally. Sometimes, though, a mutation—a change in the DNA of a cell—occurs because of hereditary factors or a carcinogen (something in the environment), or both. When this happens, there are three possible outcomes for a mutated cell. First, it may die and simply be replaced. Second, the mutation may allow the cell to continue doing the job it's meant to do, such as make breast milk. Or third, it can replicate itself over and over, replete with its errors. This collection of wacky cells forms a tumor.

As Dr. Love explains, though, this isn't enough to create cancer. The naughty cells must live among other cells (e.g., blood, fat, immune). As long as this community of cells does what they are supposed to, they will have a good influence on the mutated cell, which will coexist peacefully with them, and no disease will occur. But if this community of cells stimulates or tolerates the mutated cell's bad behavior, poof! The tumor will be cancerous. 4

Malignant (cancerous) cells can travel to other parts of the body through lymph nodes or blood. If the breast cancer cells metastasize—meaning spread and are detected in other organs, such as the liver— the tumor at the new site is still considered breast cancer (and not liver cancer, for example). Treatment strategies are discussed in chapter 2.

Diagnostic tests

Your friend saw a specialist because something wasn't quite right. Perhaps she or her partner felt a lump in her breast, or noticed some dimpling, swelling, nipple pain, or nipple discharge. Maybe her primary care physician or gynecologist noticed something suspicious during a routine examination. Or perhaps she had a mammogram or other breast imaging (such as an MRI or ultrasound), and the results warranted further testing. However she arrived on the specialist's doorstep, she's likely to undergo some of the following procedures to determine if the tumor is malignant:

- **Fine needle aspiration (FNA)**: a very thin, hollow needle is inserted into the tumor and a small sample of cells is withdrawn. If the lump can't be felt, the doctor may use an ultrasound to help guide the needle to the correct location. A pathologist will examine the fluid or tissue sample to determine if there is a malignancy. If the results aren't clear or the doctor is still suspicious, a core needle biopsy may be conducted.

- **Core needle biopsy**: is similar to the fine needle aspiration, only uses a bigger needle and takes a small cylinder of tissue from the tumor. As with the FNA, an ultrasound may be used to guide the needle to the group of suspicious cells. Sometimes a stereotactic biopsy is done whereby computers target the exact location of the tumor using mammograms taken from two angles. 5 These procedures are done with a local anesthetic in an outpatient setting and are more likely to provide a clear diagnosis than a fine needle aspiration.

- **Mammotome® and ATEC® (Automated Tissue Excision and Collection)**: are vacuum-assisted biopsies in which a tissue sample is taken from the suspicious area with a hollow probe. Once the skin has been anesthetized, a small cut is made, and the probe is guided to the suspicious area with the help of imaging (ultrasound, MRI, or x-ray). A rotating knife within the probe cuts a cylinder of tissue from the breast and is suctioned out. 6 An advantage of this procedure is that several samples can be taken from the incision site. As with core needle biopsies, vacuum-assisted biopsies are done in an outpatient setting.

- **ABBI (Advanced Breast Biopsy Instrument)**: as with the Mammotome® and ATEC®, the ABBI uses a probe with a rotating knife (as well as a heated electric wire) to remove a large sample of tissue from the breast. ABBI excises more tissue—both healthy and suspicious— than other core biopsies. Afterwards, a few stitches are often required and the procedure generally leaves a small scar. 7

- **Excisional biopsy**: is the removal of the entire tumor and surrounding margin of normal-looking tissue. This is an outpatient procedure done under local anesthesia or conscious sedation, and may be the only surgery that is needed. At the very least, it will likely offer an accurate diagnosis. Stitches are required, and the procedure generally leaves a scar.

- **Lumpectomy**: is an excisional biopsy taken one

step further, with the sampling of lymph nodes near the breast. In the past, surgeons removed at least ten nodes in a procedure called axillary node dissection or axillary sampling. In recent years, however, doctors discovered that this may not be necessary. Instead, a sentinel node biopsy will tell the surgeon if cancer has spread to the lymph nodes. After dye is injected into the tumor site, the surgeon watches which group of lymph nodes it travels to. The first node, called the sentinel node, is removed and examined under a microscope. Because lymph nodes are linear, if the sentinel node is clean of cancer, no additional lymph node surgery is required. Some surgeons may excise a few more nodes to be safe, although it is highly unlikely that cancer would be found in nodes that drain after the sentinel node. Typically when cancer cells are found in the sentinel node, though, the standard of care is to excise the remaining nodes in the area (axillary node dissection) to help determine the extent to which the cancer has spread. However, new research suggests that full lymph node removal may be unnecessary in early cancers, due to similar survival rates between groups who had a sentinel node removal versus full node removal. [8]

The cancer diagnosis

This is the nerve-wracking moment your friend has been waiting for. Of course, the best case scenario is that the tumor is benign. If she is diagnosed with breast cancer, however, she'll be inundated with more medical terms than she ever wanted to hear.

Most breast cancers can be divided into two groups, non-invasive (carcinoma in situ) and invasive. Below is an explanation for each, with treatment strategies discussed in chapter 2.

Noninvasive breast cancer

Ductal carcinoma in situ (or DCIS) refers to cancer cells that are confined to the ducts and have not invaded other breast tissue or traveled to other organs in the body. Similarly, lobular carcinoma in situ (or LCIS) refers to cancer cells that are within the milk-producing lobules. Although contained, DCIS is more likely to grow into an invasive cancer than LCIS. LCIS is a precancerous lesion, with an extremely low probability of becoming an invasive cancer. Its presence is primarily an indication that there's an increased risk of developing cancer in both breasts. The good news, however, is that nearly all women diagnosed with DCIS and LCIS can be cured. DCIS and LCIS account for approximately 5% of all breast cancers.

Invasive breast cancer

Invasive breast cancers mean that the cancer has broken through the wall of the ducts (invasive ductal carcinoma, or IDC) or the lobules (invasive lobular carcinoma, or ILC); (see Figure 1.2). Once breast cancer is invasive, it may be able to metastasize to other organs via the lymph nodes or bloodstream.

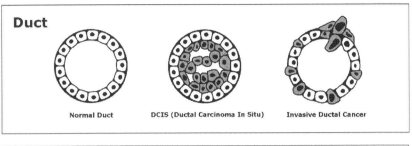

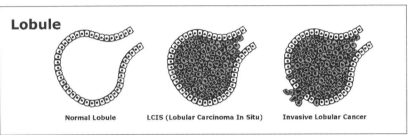

Figure 1.2

Most breast cancers are invasive ductal carcinomas (70%), whereas invasive lobular carcinomas comprise 10% of diagnoses. 9 Discussion of other, rare breast cancers (which are often variations on invasive ductal carcinoma), may be found in Dr. Susan Love's Breast Book. 10

Understanding the pathology report

A pathology report can be intimidating, but if you're familiar with the jargon, it becomes easier to understand. The information gathered during excision of a tumor, breast tissue, and lymph nodes helps determine the breast cancer stage and treatment strategies.

Some key aspects of the pathology report include the following:

- **Diagnosis**: This is the pathologist's summary diagnosis and may include information about all of the tumor's characteristics.

- **Location**: Where the cancer started, either in the lobes or the ducts of the breast.

- **Non-invasive versus invasive**: Whether the cancer is non-invasive (the cells have not spread from the point of origin) or invasive (the cells have grown past the point of origin and invaded surrounding tissue).

- **Size**: The size of the tumor, usually measured in centimeters. The area indicates where the cancer cells were present, not the entire biopsy.

- **Tumor grade**: Refers to how different the shapes of the cancer cells are compared to normal breast cells. Grade 1, or well differentiated, refers to cells that look like normal cells and usually grow slowly. Grade 2, or moderately differentiated, look somewhat different than normal cells and often grow faster. Poorly differentiated, or Grade 3, are irregular in shape and tend to grow more aggressively and quickly than normal breast cells.

- **Nuclear grade**: Refers to how closely the cancer cells' nuclei (the central part of the cell) look like normal breast cells. As with tumor grade, the higher the nuclear grade, the more abnormal and aggressive the cells are.

- **Staging**: Refers to the extent of the cancer's spread within the breast, to lymph nodes, nearby tissue, and other organs (a comprehensive review of the staging system may be found in the "Staging" section of this chapter).

- **Margin**: To be certain that all of the cancer has been removed, a surgeon will cut out extra tissue surrounding the tumor. A margin is the outer surface of the tissue sample that was removed. In a pathology report, margins are referred to as negative, close, or positive. Specifically, a negative margin is free of cancer cells, whereas a close margin indicates that cancer cells are present and near to (but not out to) the outer edge of the tissue sample. A positive margin means that cancer cells are out to the edge of the tissue sample and that some cancer cells have been left behind in the breast. 11

- **Lymph node involvement**: Negative lymph node status means that no cancer cells were found in the lymph nodes that were excised. Positive lymph node status indicates cancer cells are present.

- **Hormone-receptor status**: This tells us whether breast cancer cells are estrogen and/or progesterone positive or negative. Some breast cancer cells need estrogen and/or progesterone to grow, and are referred to as estrogen-receptor positive (ER positive) or progesterone-receptor positive (PR positive). Cancer cells that do not need these female hormones to develop are called ER negative and PR negative. A percentage is usually given that indicates the number of breast cancer cells that were positive or negative for the hormone receptors (i.e., 97% estrogen receptive). This information has long-term treatment implications, discussed in chapter 3.

- **HER2/neu status (human epidermal growth factor receptor):** Refers to a gene that indicates how quickly the cancer cells are growing. It produces HER2 receptors, which direct how quickly the cells divide—the more receptors, the faster the cells grow. Knowing the Her2/neu status is important because 1) Her2/neu positive tumors tend to be more aggressive, and 2) as with hormone receptor status, a negative or positive reading will guide a physician's treatment plan.

  Two common tests for the Her2/neu gene include the IHC (immunohistochemistry) and the FISH (fluorescence in situ hybridization). IHC indicates how much HER2/neu protein was found on the cancer cell's surface, with scores of 0, +1, +2, or +3 (0 or +1 means that the tumor is HER2/neu-negative; +2 indicates that the results are unclear; and +3 means the tumor is HER2/neu-positive). If the result is +2 or higher, confirmation can be made with fluorescence in situ hybridization. FISH detects how many copies of the HER2/neu gene are in the cancer cells, and yields a HER2/neu-positive or HER2/neu-negative result. 12

Additional diagnostic tests

If the pathology report confirms lymph node involvement, other diagnostic tests will be ordered. These play a critical role in determining if the cancer has spread to other organs.

- **Bone scans**: with the aid of low-level radioactive material, cameras detect "hot spots" or areas on the skeleton that suggest cancer activity.

- **CT scan (Computed Tomography)**: with the aid of contrast solution or dye, cross-sectional images of the body are taken by a special x-ray. A computer then combines these images into picture slices of the area in question. For breast cancer, this test is most often used to look at the chest and/or abdomen to see if the cancer has spread to other organs. 13

- **PET scan (Positron Emission Tomography)**: glucose that contains a radioactive atom is injected into the bloodstream, and because cancer cells grow rapidly, they absorb large amounts of the radioactive sugar. After about an hour, a special camera is used to create a picture of radioactive areas in the body. A PET scan is helpful when a doctor suspects that cancer may have spread but doesn't know where. [14]

- **MRI (Magnetic Resonance Imaging)**: MRI scans use radio waves and strong magnets instead of x-rays. The energy from the radio waves is absorbed and then released in a pattern formed by the type of body tissue and certain diseases. With the help of contrast material injected before the scan, a computer translates the pattern into a very detailed image of body parts. [15]

- **Ultrasound**: uses sound waves and their echoes to produce a picture of internal organs or masses. A small microphone-like instrument called a transducer sends out sound waves and picks up the echoes as they bounce off body tissues. The echoes are converted by a computer into a black and white image that is shown on the computer screen. [16] Transvaginal ultrasounds are used to look for suspicious masses in the ovaries and uterus, while abdominal ultrasounds are utilized for organs in the abdominal area, including the liver.

Genetic testing
Tests are often ordered for the breast cancer

genes BRCA1 and BRCA2, and the results may or may not impact treatment strategies. Genetic testing is a slippery slope. Although the majority of hereditary breast cancers can be attributed to mutations in the BRCA1 and BRCA2 genes, not all women who test positive for the genes will develop breast cancer. Conversely, there are many women (like me) who are not carriers of the gene but still get breast cancer.

With that said, a positive result means a higher risk of developing cancer in the "good" breast, having a recurrence in the "bad" breast, or being diagnosed with other female cancers, such as ovarian. [17] Because of this, some women choose proactive or aggressive treatment strategies, such as a prophylactic bilateral mastectomy (removal of both breasts) or an oophorectomy (removal of ovaries). Others, however, are more comfortable with a "wait and see" approach. It's a highly personal choice, with many variables factoring into the decision.

MammaPrint is a test for early-stage breast cancer that analyzes critical genes integral in developing a metastasis. [18] The results place patients in two distinct groups, either low risk or high risk for distant recurrence. As with the BRCA1 and BRCA2 tests, results may have implications for treatment strategies.

Oncotype DX is another early-stage breast cancer test that may guide treatment decisions. By analyzing twenty-one different genes from the tumor, pathologists can assess the likelihood of recurrence within 10 years of the original diagnosis, as well as the responsiveness of breast cancer tissue to chemotherapy. [19] Specifically, if a recurrence score is low, hormone therapy may be sufficient treatment; a high score, however, indicates that chemotherapy may be most beneficial.

Staging

Before being diagnosed with breast cancer, I thought staging was a simple system. It's not, at least to me. As an example, stages two and three have multiple levels—so not all stage two (or stage three) breast cancers are created equal.

The most common classification system is the TNM, short for Tumor (its size), Nodes (the number of lymph nodes involved), and Metastasis (whether the cancer has spread and can be detected in other organs). This, along with other indicators (such as the cancer cells' rate of growth) will determine a patient's treatment plan.

Below are the various stages of breast cancer and the conditions that must be met in each category: [20]

- **Stage 0**: This is a pre-cancerous condition, found either in the ducts of the breast (ductal carcinoma in situ, or DCIS), or the lobes of the breast (lobular carcinoma in situ, or LCIS).

- **Stage 1A**: The tumor is 2 centimeters or smaller, with no lymph node involvement, nor any metastasis.

- **Stage 1B**: The tumor is 2 centimeters or smaller, but the sentinel node(s) have micrometastases

(i.e., 0.2 to 2 millimeters)

- **Stage 2A**: The tumor is 2 centimeters or smaller and has spread to 1 to 3 axillary lymph nodes (under the arm),

OR

the tumor is between 2 and 5 centimeters but hasn't spread to the axillary lymph nodes,

OR

no tumor is found in the breast but cancer is in 1 to 3 axillary lymph nodes.

- **Stage 2B**: The tumor is between 2 and 5 centimeters and has spread to 1 to 3 axillary lymph nodes,

OR

the tumor is larger than 5 centimeters but has not gone into the axillary lymph nodes.

- **Stage 3A**: The tumor is 5 centimeters or smaller and has spread to 4 to 9 axillary lymph nodes that are attached to each other or other struc-tures,
OR

the tumor is bigger than 5 centimeters and has

spread to 1 to 9 axillary lymph nodes that may or may not be attached to each other and other structures,

OR

no tumor is found in the breast but the cancer is in 4 to 9 axillary lymph nodes that are attached to each other or to other structures.

- **Stage 3B**: The tumor can be any size and has gone into the tissue near the breast, such as the chest muscles and ribs,

AND

may be in 0 to 9 lymph nodes within the breast or under the arm.

- **Stage 3C**: The tumor can be any size, and 10 or more of the lymph nodes under the arm are affected

OR

cancer is in the lymph nodes beneath the collarbone or above the collarbone on the cancerous breast side,

OR

cancer is in the lymph nodes near the sternum

and armpit

- **Stage 4**: The tumor can be any size, with any lymph node involvement, and has spread to other organs in the body, most often the bones, liver, lung, and brain.

What does all of this mean?

During the time of a breast cancer diagnosis, your friend will be deluged with medical information. Like me, it'll make her head spin, at least a little. But it's important that she, as well as her loved ones, have a rudimentary understanding of her diagnostic tests and pathology report. Her doctors are detectives, and every test result is a piece of the puzzle in getting well. Each bit of information is the basis for short- and long-term treatment strategies, many of which will be discussed in chapters two and three.

How to help her early on: What to say, not to say, and acts of kindness

Suggestions on what to say

I'm not sure what's worse, being the one to break bad news or the one who has to hear it. For some, the words may come easily when offering support and comfort to a friend who's been diagnosed. Perhaps you know exactly what she needs to hear in that moment. Other friends, however, may struggle. My best advice is to simply *let your friend know that you'll be there to go on this journey with her, and that she won't have to face her illness alone.*

If you're at a loss for words, go ahead and say so. There's nothing wrong with, *"I don't know what to say"* or *"I'm sorry."* Don't feel pressured to come up with something profound in these moments. A simple *"I'm here for you,"* or *"I'm thinking about you"* goes a long, long way in comforting us. We know that for many friends and loved ones, it's difficult to be silent after hearing bad news. As a result, silly, spontaneous comments are often made out of fear or nervousness. We also know that we've had a bit of time to process this turn of events. You haven't.

Trust that you know your friend well enough to recognize what she needs at any given time. If she's not in the mood to talk today, it doesn't mean that she won't be up for hearing from you the next day. Don't take it personally and think that you can't reach out again, or that you have to wait to hear from her.

When I was in the middle of my surgeries and months and months of chemotherapy, I didn't have the energy or inclination to chase people down, nor did I think it was my responsibility. Please don't make your friend feel like she needs to be the one to reach out now—she may not have the energy, and even if she does, she might be afraid to drag you down if she's having a bad day. Conversely, she may not want to talk to anyone if all people ever ask about is the disease. She may want to take a break from the cancer talk and feel normal. Again, this is why you need to pay attention to her cues and trust that you know her well enough to extend kindness in the most appropriate form. Simply ask if there's anything she does or does not feel like talking about.

Diagnosis

Just as best friends come in all shapes and sizes, so do patients. Recognize that there may be cultural and economic differences among those fighting breast cancer (immigrant versus non-immigrant, for example). Unfortunately, some women suffer silently. Despite our differences, we are all fragile and fearful to some extent, and appreciate compassion from those around us. Know that support comes in many forms—a hug, a letter, or even silence. Your friend's need for love and kindness may never be greater than it is now.

Through word of mouth and during breast cancer walks, I met survivors who graciously agreed to be interviewed (both in person and online) for this book. They shared their experiences and thoughts on a number of subjects, including what to say and not to say during all stages of the illness, as well as acts of kindness that meant the world to them. Below are sentiments they found inspiring and touching when first diagnosed (note that some participants wanted to be identified, others did not):

"I love you." --Anonymous, age 52

"I love you very much and we're going to get through this together." --Dorothy G., age 69

"You are beautiful and strong." --Gwen C., age 49

"You uplift everyone around you." --Carolyn G., age 53

"I am here for you, I am here for the long haul, and I want you with me." --Kimberly B., age 55

"You're going to beat this, stay strong, we love you." --Deanna R., age 47

"I'm proud of you." --Anonymous

"You're an inspiration to me." --Anonymous

"Constantly calling me an inspiration — made me want to do well for myself and for them." --Sheryl R., age 42

Again, it's okay to show your own vulnerability with this news. Honest to goodness, we would rather that you hem and haw and trip over your words than not reach out at all. If you're confused, scared, and nervous, tell us. It's alright. If the most you can muster in those first moments is a hand squeeze or a hug, know that many times those gestures say something more important than any human can adequately articulate anyway. There's nothing wrong with sitting in silence. One 40 year-old survivor said, *"I liked having people come over to sit with me and knowing that they didn't have to talk — just be there."* I agree. I love that with the people I'm closest to, we can be in each other's presence, relaxed, content, and grateful to just "be."

If you want to talk, though, another suggestion for a communication boost is asking questions, as long as your friend seems receptive to this type of conversation. Dating experts recommend that when getting to know someone, you should avoid questions that yield simple, one-word answers. I think the same can be said here. Perhaps instead of phrasing it as, *"Are you scared?"* you could ask how your friend is feeling (about the diagnosis, who she will share the news with, how, etc.). It's a subtle difference, but give her the door and space to expound on what she's experiencing.

What not to say (or at least be wary of)

As mentioned before, I think that most women dealing with breast cancer would rather that you just reach out, even if you say something that may be construed (unknowingly) as impolite or lacking compassion. We understand that this is a difficult and awkward time for you, too. The reality is that many hurtful comments come from a place of nervousness, fear, and ignorance. Still, I believe that most people are well-intentioned, even if what creeps out of their mouths sounds thoughtless.

With that said, below are some comments that I (and other breast cancer survivors) found irritating or upsetting when we were diagnosed. Simply put, we'd like you to be cognizant that there may be a better way to express certain sentiments.

What annoyed me most during this stage was when someone would say, *"Ah, you'll be fine."* Counter-intuitive, huh? You might assume that this is exactly what someone wants to hear (and of course, some actually do). But for me and many others, it comes across as extremely flippant and thoughtless.

That comment—especially the way in which it's delivered—can disregard the gravity of the situation and our feelings, including genuine fear.

Upon hearing my news, a good friend said, *"Aahh, you'll be fine. My aunt just had breast cancer last year and she's fine."* What irked me was that my own doctor didn't even know the seriousness of my condition and wasn't making any bold statements yet, so why should anyone else? To cut him some slack, I know it was an awkward moment. He probably felt pressured to say something encouraging and uplifting. But it's more important to take a breath and not worry about saying something clever, profound, or too Pollyanna-ish. Sometimes lightning-quick reassurances have the opposite effect you're going for.

Also, let your friend talk and vent without trying to be Little Miss (or Mr.) Fix It. My closest male friend explained that this is particularly difficult for many men, who tend to be problem solvers and want to "fix things." Some breast cancer survivors explained that this was annoying, even if it was coming from a well-meaning place. Don't push advice or suggestions. If she wants your input, she'll ask, and even then she may not follow through on what you've proposed. Don't take it personally—she has a lot to sort out.

When asked which comments were hurtful, annoying, stupid, ignorant/thoughtless, and wished they hadn't heard when diagnosed, some breast cancer survivors generated the following list:

"I had breast cancer "x" number of years ago and

I'm still here. You will be fine." --Jan K., age 59

"One of my co-workers told me upon hearing that I had cancer was 'Your body is just a shell,' making me feel like I was going to die soon." --Anonymous, age 61

"Smoking cancer sticks did this." --Anonymous, age 52

"It seems everyone wanted to share their experience with losing someone from one form of cancer or another. The last thing I wanted to hear was about the death of friends and family." --Barb C., age 52

"Many people had stories of family members that died—didn't need to hear it and avoided negative energy." --Sheryl R., age 42

"My father in-law's new wife had breast cancer so she continued to share her 'horror' stories with me unsolicited all the while claiming she is so positive about everything." --JZ, age 47

"The first words out of my sister's mouth were 'great, so now my chances of getting breast cancer are higher.' The second time I was diagnosed my other sister said, 'I hope you're adopted, or I hope I'm adopted' (referring to the genetics of this)." --Anonymous, age 56

Others to be wary of...

"I know exactly how you feel." Unless you've been through it, you don't. And even if you have had

a similar diagnosis, each person's experience is unique. I can't possibly get into someone else's head and feel exactly what she's feeling, nor could anyone experience my journey the same way I have.

"It could be worse." Well, no shit. There's always a more dire situation and someone worse off than you. That's not the point. This is your friend's personal crisis and shouldn't be trivialized. Along that same line: *"Be grateful that it's not ____."* Someone said to me, *"Be thankful that it's not ovarian cancer, because that's much worse."* None of it's a picnic, so there's no need to pit cancers against each other and play the comparison game. (Note: one breast cancer survivor told me that once, when she was feeling very sorry for herself, a friend reminded her that she could be dead. She explains, *"Though this could be considered harsh, it was a truthful reminder of what I had to be grateful for."* This is a good example of needing to know the person you're talking to, because personally, I'd want to smack someone making a remark like that. But for this survivor, it was what she needed to hear in that moment to shift her perspective.)

"This is happening for a reason." Maybe. But it's up to the woman with breast cancer to go on that personal journey and figure it out, and to make sense of what's happening without lots of interpretations from others. Along that same line: *"God has a plan,"* *"It's in God's hands,"* *"God knows what he's doing."* If you're good friends with someone, you're likely to know where she falls on the religion spectrum. Even if someone is spiritual, not everyone wants to hear the God talk right now. Remember, your friend may be

angry at a higher power and some of these sentiments can come off as platitudes.

"None of us knows how long we have" or *"I could get hit by a bus tomorrow."* And? This is annoying because not only is it stating the obvious, but it can be filed under flippant comments that don't acknowledge our fear and what we're going through. We're dealing with the here and now and don't need to speculate on when the next "bus" is going to take us out.

"Be positive," "Have a good attitude," et. al. Oh, yuck! Ever notice how when you're in a bad mood and someone says, *"Don't be in a bad mood"* it makes you even uglier? Telling someone to look on the bright side or to be positive right now sounds exasperatingly shallow. If she's going to be strong and upbeat after a breast cancer diagnosis, it'll come from within—not because someone is in her ear telling her what to do or how to be.

"You really should get into a support group." Support groups can be wonderfully nurturing and a lifeline for some. As Gail N., a 57 year-old breast cancer survivor explained, *"Joining breastcancer2@ yahoogroups. com was the best! Much better to associate with those who truly understand what you're going through."* Honestly, though, they're not for everyone. Michele R., 46, shared that *"For me, my breast cancer was a private journey. Only in the most recent years have I been able to share my experience. I am over 5 years now, and I can talk comfortably about my cancer. At the time, I wasn't the kind of patient who wanted the bells and whistles of walks and fellowship of others."* Personally, I wasn't

opposed to attending a meeting, but I already had a strong social network that enveloped me in all the love and warmth I felt I needed. Each person must decide for herself. Instead of telling your friend that she needs to sign up, ask her, *"Do you think a support group would be beneficial?"* or *"Have you thought about looking into support groups?"* Phrasing it this way is kinder, gentler.

"What did the doctor say about your prognosis?" Wow, this one just sounds bad, as if your friend's been given a death sentence and you're asking for the physician's wager on the day it's going to happen. This isn't Vegas. I can't think of a time when someone with a breast cancer diagnosis would want to hear this. As her friend, of course you want to know how this story will unfold, but for many of us, "prognosis" is a scary word and can tie us up in knots. As Freddie B., a 62 year-old survivor explained, *"There is no way to express the fear that comes with this disease."* Be careful to avoid comments or questions that will frighten your friend even more than she already is.

Acts of kindness

During the diagnosis phase, communication is at the very top of the kindness to do list. Extending your love and support through cards, letters, emails, and phone calls (and visits, if she's up for them) mean so much when your friend is feeling shell-shocked. Having the wagons circle 'round will give her much-needed strength to move toward the treatment stage. Some breast cancer survivors explain below:

Diagnosis

"Phone calls from friends were very helpful...friends from out of state, friends I had not heard from for a long time...I had so many people rally to my support. It stopped me from sinking deeper into a depression that I know would have become fatal." --Kimberly B., age 55

"My parents and dearest friend are 1000 miles away, but they found time to call. These calls were the highlight of my day and helped remind me of my strength and the strength of the support team I had in place." --Michele R., age 46

"I have received many cards from family and friends. It means so much to know that others are thinking of me and wishing me well." --Deanna R., age 47

"Friends called on the telephone, sent fun cards and meaningful verses, and asked what books I liked to read, and bought a book I had not yet read." --Anonymous, age 66

"I am especially grateful for the hundreds of calls I received, so many that I eventually had to keep my phone mailbox full!" –Deena B., 41

"A friend gave me a journal with a message that said, 'You were meant to walk this journey.'" --Anonymous

"I received very few phone calls, but those I got were really appreciated." --Carolyn G., age 53

The following are acts of kindness breast cancer

survivors found especially meaningful during this stage of their illness. For our purposes, simply substitute husband, boyfriend, mother, sister, etc. with "friend."

Household

This includes food (cooking, grocery shopping, take-out, gift certificates to restaurants); housework/ laundry; yard work; and caregiving for children and/or pets.

"When I was first diagnosed, my husband's best friend gathered 8 other friends to come over and do yard work. They spent the good part of their Saturday in our front and back yard (we live on 1.6 acres). This allowed my husband the opportunity to take over some of my inside tasks without having the weight of responsibility for the yard work hanging over his head. I set up a helping hands website for people to volunteer to bring food and clean the house. We had 3 meals a week delivered by friends. What a wonderful thing they did for us. I was busy fighting cancer (boy, that makes you TIRED!!), my husband was doing what I normally did, and our kids took up some slack as well. It was really nice to know that making dinner didn't have to be one of the responsibilities on my hubby's plate as well. My mother set up an every-other-week housecleaning session and some of my BUNCO group came over and gave the house a good cleaning as well." --Anonymous, age 40

"Friends brought over pizza after first finding out. Just meant so much that these friends cared and knew I would not be cooking (or eating, but would need support, as

well as my husband). My father in-law brought over meals, as well as friends. While on this journey you do not feel like cooking but must eat, as well as your family." --Gwen C., age 49

Logistics

This includes research about any aspect of the illness; organizing / filing / copying paperwork (medical, insurance); offering to be the point person / disseminator of information about your friend; driving her to medical appointments or other errands; attending medical appointments with her and offering to take notes; and helping with tasks in the workplace.

"My best friends did a lot of research for me as soon as I was diagnosed because they wanted me to have as much information as possible to make appropriate decisions regarding treatment. At first all of the information they provided me with was overwhelming, but I later appreciated their efforts. My brother and boyfriend took turns driving me to my many medical appointments. My boyfriend took notes and asked questions for me because I was too over-whelmed and depressed to do so." --Isabel N., age 35

"My sisters would go to most of my doctor visits with me and take notes, as info would go in one ear and out the other for me." --Anonymous, age 61

"My stepdad has been my main support during this difficult time. He has been to every appointment, has done research, and been so patient." --Deanna R., age 47

"My family provided research and love." --Sheryl R., age 42

"My husband was with me for all of my appointments, as well as my mother. Although I had done most of the research myself, they would sit down with me ahead of time and go over my information and the questions that I had so to make sure that they understood and could be sure I got the answers to my questions. I honestly don't remember most of the initial months of diagnosis—they were my mind and heart when I could not function." --Kimberly B., age 55

"My daughter did research about my cancer and about the type of treatment that I was going to receive. My husband took me to all of my appointments. My husband is also keeping track of all the medical bills. It took all of the worry off of my shoulders and all I had to worry about was getting better." --Dorothy G., age 69

"A cousin who had breast cancer prior to me gave me books and information." --Anonymous, age 56

"Having my husband and daughter attend appointments (and radiation sessions) with me made the process seem more 'normal' than when I was alone. We even found humor in the most serious of situations, which made it all the more tolerable." --Pink Warrior, age 55

"My sister in-law offered to take notes, but my husband is very good at it." --Gwen C., age 49

"My friend did research that she chose not to share because of the content, but I know she spent many evenings looking up information and crying." --Anonymous, age 40

"My husband attended all of my important appointments with me." --Anonymous

An extended list of acts of kindness and suggestions on how to help your friend may be found in the next chapter, because it is during the treatment phase that loved ones can be especially helpful.

Support for you

As mentioned before, those of us fighting cancer know that this is an extremely difficult time for you, too. It's not just the patient who needs support! One of my wisest, dearest friends reminded me that there is a ripple effect of emotions and fears after a cancer diagnosis. She explained that during my illness, she relied heavily on her support system. Reaching out may be particularly important for men in order to avoid isolation. Although traditionally criticized for showing "weakness," they, too, need a healthy dose of compassion. Bottom line, be strong for your friend with breast cancer, but have someone who will be a source of strength for you, too.

Chapter 2
Treatment

What your friend may be thinking

For the women I've talked to, this stage is characterized by two streams of thought: nervousness about treatment and empowerment to face the disease head on. This is the getting-down-to-business phase, which can be a welcome change from the waiting game that comes after initial testing and diagnosis.

There's a wide range of fear going into treatment; your friend may be slightly unsettled or extremely frightened. Whatever she's feeling is normal and valid. The good news is that if she finds herself in trepidation's clutches, she'll soon learn that oftentimes, the anticipation of (fill in the blank: surgery, losing her hair) is much worse than the actual thing she fears. I was warned by a number of people that chemotherapy would be the most horrible thing I'd ever have to endure. Admittedly, it was no joyride. But for me, at least, it wasn't the nightmare that I had anticipated, either. Same thing with my hair: oh, how I dreaded losing it, but wasn't traumatized when it happened like I thought I would be. Still, surgery, radiation, and chemotherapy are all serious treatment strategies, so no one should begrudge that pit in your friend's stomach.

The exciting aspect of the treatment phase is the sense of empowerment many women feel. Your friend and her doctors are a tag team taking on this unwelcome adversary, each doing their part to wipe out the S.O.B. Even if she isn't the one performing surgery or administering drugs, your friend is taking charge of her health. Perhaps she's eating well, getting plenty of rest, or following all of her doctors' orders to a T. She's doing something, which feels better than being a passive participant in the fight of her life. What if she's making a choice that you don't agree with? Remember that as her friend, your role is to support, not judge.

Understanding her medical options

Before discussing your friend's medical treatments, here's a list of key people who will be critical in helping her get well. Meet the all-star team:

- **Breast surgeon:** this person specializes in all breast surgeries, whether removal of a tumor or the entire breast and lymph nodes. This doctor either does breast surgery exclusively or is a general surgeon who has a great deal of experience in surgical breast procedures. Or your friend may have a surgical oncologist, who specializes in removing cancerous tumors.

- **Plastic surgeon**: for those who choose to have reconstruction after a mastectomy, this person specializes in creating a new breast. The reconstruction may happen immediately after the mastectomy, in which case (s)he works closely with the breast surgeon, or it may take place at some point in the future. It's the patient's choice. If reconstruction occurs right after the mastectomy, the plastic surgeon is in charge of your friend's follow-up care (as I was told, "Whoever works on you last is in charge of your aftercare"). Generally, your friend will see the plastic surgeon once a week for about three weeks following the surgery to assess how she's healing. In addition, her drains, which are the plastic tubes placed in her chest to gather tissue fluid, will be removed. My plastic surgeon wanted to meet with me several months later, too, to see the final outcome of the reconstruction and answer any of my questions.

- **Radiation oncologist**: this person is in charge of your friend's radiation treatments. His or her goal is to eradicate any cancer cells left behind while limiting damage to the healthy cells and tissue in the breast.

- **Medical oncologist**: if chemotherapy is required, this is the person who will oversee the treatment program. (S)he is the cancer expert and will determine which chemical therapies (e.g., "chemo" drugs, such as Taxotere, Cytoxan, etc.) or hormonal therapies (e.g., Tamoxifen) should be administered, in what combination, and for how long. Someone gave me this bit of advice soon after my diagnosis and it was 100% true: your friend should have an excellent rapport with this specialist, because (s)he will be her lead doctor (seeing him/her every three months) for several years. Your friend should feel like her oncologist is her number one ally and always looking out for her. Mine makes me feel completely safe and secure, and I trust him implicitly. I can't imagine going on this journey without him.

- **Gynecologist**: your friend's gynecologist should be in the loop during her treatment, meaning good communication between doctors and medical records shared. Her gynecologist will be involved in discussions regarding any "hormonal" issues (e.g., if chemotherapy has kicked your friend into menopause, managing menopausal symptoms, etc.). Also, because breast cancer is closely related to other female cancers such as ovarian, her gynecologist should keep a close eye on your friend for the first few years with regular examinations and transvaginal ultrasounds.

Surgeries

When a woman is diagnosed with breast cancer,

she can count on having a surgical procedure, however minor or major, as part of her treatment plan. Removal of the tumor(s) is most often the first step in dealing with the enemy.

Lumpectomy

As mentioned in the previous chapter, a lumpectomy removes the entire tumor and a surrounding margin of normal-looking tissue. In addition, a sentinel node biopsy is performed and tells the surgeon if cancer has spread to the lymph nodes. If the sentinel node is clean of cancer, no additional lymph node surgery is required; however, some surgeons may excise a few more nodes to be safe. If cancer cells are found in the sentinel node, however, the remaining nodes in the area are typically excised (axillary node dissection) to help determine the extent to which the cancer has spread (note that as discussed in chapter one, new research suggests that a full node dissection may not be necessary in stage one and two cancers).

This surgery takes approximately two to three hours under general anesthesia, plus a few hours in the recovery room, and is usually done on an outpatient basis. She'll need someone to drive her home from the hospital or surgery center and stay with her the first day/night. Also, she'll be uncomfortable and sore, but the pain can be managed with medication. Her upper body mobility will be limited and she may feel icky from the anesthesia. Your friend will also have stitches, and the procedure generally leaves a scar. However, this isn't called breast-conserving surgery for nothing. My talented breast surgeon, Dr. Kristi Funk, did such an incredible job that you'd barely know that I had a chunk of my breast removed. In my case, it wasn't enough to eliminate the cancer completely, but the outcome of the initial surgery was beautiful.

Possible side effects of a lumpectomy include swelling, tenderness, buildup of blood or clear fluid in the excised area, scar tissue, and infection.

Mastectomy and bilateral mastectomy

A mastectomy is the removal of all breast tissue (in the case of bilateral, both breasts). A *simple* or *total* mastectomy refers to a procedure in which the entire breast (including the nipple) is removed, but the lymph nodes and muscle under the breast are left intact. A *modified radical mastectomy* removes the entire breast and axillary lymph nodes. A *radical mastectomy* removes the entire breast, axillary lymph nodes, and the muscles under the breast. This procedure was once common but rarely performed today, because the modified radical mastectomy is just as effective without the additional side effects and disfigurement.

These procedures take several hours under general anesthesia, particularly if reconstruction is done right after. A hospital stay of a few days is generally required. Your friend will feel like a ton of bricks is piled on top of her chest, and she may have difficulty breathing at first. Her nurses will encourage her to practice breathing deeply as much as she can tolerate it. Heavy-duty pain medication is administered after the surgery, which may make your friend nauseous, dizzy, and loopy, and she may vomit. For some people, the residual effects of general anesthesia are known to cause these same maladies.

If your friend's experience is anything like mine, she won't be allowed to leave the hospital until she's able to show the nurses that she can keep food down. Once home, your friend will need to rest for a couple of weeks and won't be able to lift anything for about three weeks. She'll feel very tight, stiff, and sore, but the pain is usually managed with medication.

She'll also need to record the volume of liquid in her drains, which come out of a little hole in her side and empty into a small, plastic receptacle. The tubing and plastic container stay in place with safety pins attached to a medical bra or wraparound dressing, whichever the surgeon prefers. Once there's little fluid coming out of the drains, they are removed and the bra or dressing can be changed. Many women have their drains taken out in about ten days, although mine were in place for nearly three weeks.

Possible side effects of mastectomies include pain, infection, bleeding, and lymphedema, or swelling of the arm. This occurs when the lymph nodes have been removed. Excess fluid that typically goes back into the bloodstream via lymph nodes stays in the arm, causing swelling. Lymphedema can be a short- or long-term condition. Because the breast's nerve supply has been cut, numbness in the armpit and breast area is also a long-term side effect.

Reconstruction

After the breast has been removed, many women opt for reconstructive surgery to rebuild the breast mound. This may be done right after the mastectomy, or in some cases, a woman may have to wait, or choose to have the surgery at a later time. The new breast may be constructed with artificial substances, such as saline or silicone implants, or the woman's own tissue, or both. Many women must have expanders placed under the muscle during a mastectomy in order to stretch the tissue. The expanders are inflated over time with saline until the expansion is complete, at which time the final implant, made of either saline or silicone, is placed. Some women can skip the expansion process if the skin is already stretched. At the time of my bilateral mastectomy and reconstruction, I was coming off almost ten and a half months of breastfeeding around the clock. The skin on my breasts was plenty stretched enough for immediate placement of the implants.

A new breast may also be created using the woman's own tissue, either from her abdomen (a TRAM flap, or transverse rectus abdominis muscle), her back (a latissimus dorsi flap), or her buttocks (a gluteus maximus flap). [21] The advantage of using her own tissue is that the breast achieves a more natural look, but drawbacks include a longer surgical time and recovery period. Also, in some cases, an infection at the site of tissue removal can occur if there is inadequate blood supply to the flap.

Most of the time, particularly if the tumor is large or near the nipple, the nipple and areola are not spared. Once reconstruction of the breast mound has taken place, the nipple and areola can be re-created at a later date. This is most often done with tattooing, although nipple reconstruction may be performed using the woman's own body tissue. Other women prefer to forgo nipple and areola reconstruction altogether.

Reconstruction is a highly personal choice, and all options should be carefully weighed and discussed before making a decision. Your friend may benefit from talking to others who have had successful procedures. These women, in conjunction with your friend's doctor, can answer questions and help clarify expectations about outcomes. Indeed, the surgeries are long, involved, and have potential complications immediately following the procedures and for years to come. However, the emotional and psychological boost that reconstruction offers many women cannot be discounted.

If your friend chooses not to have reconstruction, prosthetics are a viable option for many women and are covered by health insurance in several states. In addition, some charitable organizations offer free breast prosthetics to women who have had mastectomies (all4onealliance. org and pinkheartfunds.org, to name just two).

Non-invasive cancers: DCIS and LCIS

If your friend is diagnosed with ductal carcinoma in situ (DCIS), her doctor will most likely recommend a wide excision (lumpectomy), which means surgically removing the cancerous area, plus a margin of normal tissue around it. Often this is followed by radiation. If it is determined that many ducts are affected throughout the breast (multicentric) instead of just one, a mastectomy may be recommended. And if the DCIS is estrogen receptor-positive, tamoxifen (an estrogen suppressor) may be prescribed for five years to lower the risk of more DCIS or invasive cancer developing in the breasts.

Doctors typically recommend something different for LCIS. Not only does LCIS occur much less frequently than DCIS, it is also much less likely to grow into an invasive cancer. Plus, LCIS is more difficult than DCIS to pinpoint, in part because it's often multicentric (scattered throughout both breasts). In addition, LCIS forms a diffuse, single-line pattern of cells, which is more difficult to detect than clumpy, lumpy DCIS. 22 Because of these factors, most doctors often suggest close monitoring of the breasts with twice-yearly physical exams and mammograms (or MRIs) annually. The other end of the treatment spectrum is a bilateral mastectomy, which is the choice of some women who are not comfortable with the "wait and see" approach. The middle ground between these two strategies is taking the estrogen suppressor tamoxifen for five years to prevent development of breast cancer.

Radiation

Radiation is considered a local treatment because it targets cancer cells only at the tumor site. During the procedure, high energy x-rays are used to prevent cancer cells from multiplying. Although normal cells near the tumor site are also affected, they can repair themselves. The cancer cells are left reeling.

Treatment

There are two ways radiation can be given: external beam radiation and internal radiation therapy (brachytherapy). If your friend has external beam radiation, she will undergo a simulation prior to her first treatment. As she lies on a table under the radiation machine, a technician marks the area to be targeted with a special ink. These markings will stay on her skin for the entire treatment cycle and ensures that the correct area is irradiated each time. Radiation treatments last only a couple of minutes, but must be done five times a week for six to eight weeks. Side effects of the external beam radiation generally include skin changes (redness, tingling, itching, burning, and soreness), breast swelling or tenderness, and fatigue.

With internal radiation therapy, a radioactive implant is placed into or near the tumor and gives off radiation to this localized area of tissue. 23 The implant allows a higher dose of radiation to be administered to a smaller area than external beam radiation and is removed once treatment is completed (generally within 7 to 10 days). Common side effects of internal radiation therapy include discomfort or tenderness at the implant site, local skin reaction, and fatigue.

Potential long-term side effects of either radiation therapy include sore, stiff pectoral muscles and skin that is darker, less sensitive, firmer, and thicker than before treatments. Also, breasts may appear larger because of lymphedema (fluid build up) or smaller due to scar tissue.

Radiation therapy is often done after a lumpectomy to kill any cancer cells that may remain in the breast. It may also be utilized prior to surgery to shrink a tumor, or for cancer that is inoperable, or that has metastasized.

Targeted therapy

Women who have cancer that is HER2/neu positive will likely be given a drug called trastuzumab (commonly known as herceptin) once a week for a year. This treatment schedule includes several rounds of chemotherapy (herceptin goes to once every 3 weeks after cessation of chemotherapy). Trastuzumab attaches to the protein HER2/neu, which promotes cancer cell growth in approximately 20% of women diagnosed with breast cancer. [24] Because HER2/neu positive tumors tend to be more aggressive, trastuzumab is an important weapon in slowing the proliferation of cancer cells.

Trastuzumab is given as an injection, and its side effects are quite mild compared to chemotherapy. Some women experience nausea, diarrhea, fever and chills, headaches, and anemia, but typically these become less problematic after the first dose or two. The most serious potential side effect is heart damage, especially when the trastuzumab is administered along with certain chemotherapy combinations. Echocardiograms may be ordered during treatment to monitor heart function closely.

Chemotherapy

Chemotherapy is a systemic therapy because it treats the entire body, or system, and not just a local area. When administered after surgery (adjuvant chemotherapy), the goal is to kill rogue cancer cells that may have traveled to sites other than the breast. If given prior to breast surgery (neoadjuvant chemotherapy), the primary goal is to shrink the tumor before excision. In addition, chemotherapy may be the primary form of treatment when surgery cannot remove tumors or the cancer has metastasized.

Chemotherapy drugs circulate through the bloodstream and target rapidly-multiplying cancer cells. Along the way, normal cells that are also quickly-multiplying (such as in the intestinal tract and hair) are damaged as well. However, chemotherapy drugs are administered carefully in terms of frequency and dosage so that cancer cells are destroyed but normal cells bounce back. For example, a chemotherapy schedule may be every three weeks, every four weeks, or two weeks on and two weeks off. This allows the body to recover and gear up for the next round. Your friend's oncologist may recommend four, six, or eight treatments depending on her personal profile. This includes what type of breast cancer she has, how advanced it is, how well she can tolerate the treatments and manage her side effects, her overall health, and any other illnesses that must be considered. It's not a one-size-fits-all business, so everyone's regimen and combination chemotherapy (several drugs used together in varying dosages) is unique.

What is universal, though, is making sure that the patient is well enough to proceed to the next round. Blood work is done one to two days before an infusion to confirm that her body can tolerate treatment. Blood pressure, temperature, and weight are recorded as well, and the oncologist will assess any side effects she may be experiencing.

There are two ways in which the drugs may be administered, intravenously and in pill form. In most cases, a needle is inserted into a vein somewhere below the elbow, either in the hand or lower arm. The infusion typically takes between one to five hours, and your friend will be able to go home afterwards. Some people, particularly those who don't have "good" veins, receive their chemo drugs through an injection port instead. This small disc is surgically implanted under the skin and usually placed in the upper chest or upper arm.

Chemotherapy's side effects are legendary. Your friend's oncologist will prescribe medication to be taken before chemo that should ease nausea and diarrhea. In the first few days after a treatment, your friend may not feel like eating, but it's important that she get something into her system. The oncology nurses and dieticians told me that bland, starchy foods like potatoes and noodles were good choices if I felt queasy, but that they'd rather have their patients eat ice cream and chocolate milkshakes than nothing at all. (Recipes for nutritious meals that you can prepare for your friend may be found in Appendix A). Drinking a lot of water is also important during your friend's treatments because it will help flush the chemo drugs out of her system.

Other, common side effects include:

• fatigue

- blisters or sores in the mouth, throat, or on the palms of hands

- bleeding gums

- separation of fingernails from the nail bed

- a numbing or tingling feeling in the hands or feet (peripheral neuropathy), which may cause problems with balance

- hair loss (alopecia)

- "chemo brain," which can be described as a mental fogginess that affects memory, concentration, and an inability to process information

- temporary or permanent loss of menstrual cycles

- hot flashes

- infertility

And potentially more serious side effects:

- lowered red blood-cell count (anemia), which compromises the body's ability to carry oxygen throughout the body, sometimes resulting in shortness of breath and weakness

- low platelet counts, which impede the body's ability to clot blood and predisposes one to excessive bleeding and bruising

- lowered white blood-cell count (neutropenia), which can compromise the body's ability to fight infection; this is particularly important to watch because during the "dangerous" days of a chemo cycle when white blood cell counts are lowest, any infection is life-threatening

In order to stimulate bone marrow and replenish white blood cells, your friend's oncologist may want her to have a shot of granulocyte colony-stimulating factor (G-CSF) the day after her infusion or a series of shots the second week after her treatment. My G-CSF, Neulasta, was administered 24 hours after each of my treatments and caused temporary bone pain, which is a common side effect. Although not all chemotherapy patients will have G-CSF shots, I appreciated the feeling of security that Neulasta provided. Your friend's oncologist will decide what's best for her.

A critical point to make is that you must be aware of your friend's physical vulnerability during chemotherapy. This is akin to a bright, red light flashing "Warning! Warning!" The dangerous period of her chemo cycle is about a week long, and she cannot afford to be around anyone who has so much as a cold. Illnesses that she might ordinarily fight off with ease become life-threatening because of her susceptibility now. If you're not sure what her cycle is, ask. And if you're under the weather, schedule a time to see her when you're perfectly healthy.

Finally, chemotherapy strikes a chord of fear in most people, and yes, it's a very difficult treatment. But thinking about it in terms of the "big picture," I can't stress enough that it's a really wonderful ally in a cancer battle. I had a 51% chance of recurrence if I didn't do chemotherapy, whereas the likelihood of cancer returning now is only 15% thanks to completing six chemo cycles. I like those odds. If chemotherapy is recommended for your friend, my hope is that she'll feel as reassured as I was by the efficacy of this treatment.

How to help her: what to say, what not to say, and acts of kindness

Suggestions on what to say

You might think that *"Let me know if there's anything I can do"* is something every cancer patient wants to hear. And yes, in theory it sounds wonderful…but it probably isn't specific enough. A wise friend pointed this out to me while I was undergoing chemotherapy. She said, "Any time I ask you if you need anything, you always say, 'No, thanks, I'm fine.' You don't make it easy! So I'm just going to offer concrete suggestions from now on." I hadn't thought about it that way before, but she was right. I'm not the type of person who asks things of others easily, so I wasn't giving her or anyone else a chance to help. Perhaps your friend is the same way. If she is, you might want to say, *"I thought I'd bring lunch over on Thursday and do your laundry,"* or *"I have Friday morning free, would you like me to do some errands for you?"* or *"How about I bring dinner over on Wednesday night?"* or *"Would it be okay if I take your kids to the zoo on Saturday afternoon?"*

The one caveat is to ask your friend first. As an example, grocery shopping is a real chore for some people, but I love it, and when I was well, that represented an outing for me during treatment. I wouldn't have wanted anyone to do it for me.

Always legitimize her feelings. This is a critical point: no matter what she's experiencing, it's valid. Create and nurture an environment that encourages your friend to express whatever she wants. If she says, "I'm scared" say *"You have every right to be frightened"* or *"I can't imagine how scary this must be for you."* Don't be dismissive by telling her that this will all be over before she knows it or at least chemotherapy (or radiation) isn't as harsh as it used to be, or whatever. If she says, "It's not fair" say, *"No, it's not."* One of the quickest ways to give her the sense that you're in her corner is to validate her emotions.

Also, let her know that you support her decisions. After I was diagnosed, I had a lumpectomy, but it wasn't enough to remove the cancer completely. Minimally, I had to have a mastectomy. Although there was no indication that the cancer was in my other breast, my surgeon and I agreed that for me, having a prophylactic bilateral mastectomy would be a wise move. I've heard from other breast cancer survivors that this option was viewed as unnecessary and radical by some of their family members. I think that's unfortunate. Believe me, the surgery is difficult enough; I can't imagine how much more gut-wrenching it would be if you didn't have the support of loved ones and friends. Even if she's in a highly-charged, emotional state, trust that your friend is an intelligent, grown woman capable of knowing what's best for her.

Some grieving may occur now, as well as after your friend successfully completes her treatment program. Acknowledging her loss, whether it's part of a breast, one breast, or both breasts, and supporting however she needs to mourn, will always be appreciated. The night before my double mastectomy and reconstruction, I went into my bedroom and shut the door. I undressed completely and sat down in front of the mirror, staring at my breast milk-beaten boobs. "Girls," I said, "We need to talk."

Some people might think it was a kooky thing to do, but I wanted to have a heartfelt talk with my body before the big surgery. I thanked my breasts for giving me one of the most joyful experiences of my life (breastfeeding), for nourishing my baby, and providing nearly a year's worth of comfort to him. I reminisced about the first time they made an appearance (6th grade), and the many happy, fun times we shared over the years. Then I apologized for all that I had put them through in the past two years—pregnancy, breastfeeding, mammograms, needle biopsies, surgery…and that I was going to ask them to make the ultimate sacrifice for the greater good. I explained what would happen the following morning, and that these would be our last hours together. I said thank you once more, promised that I would never, ever forget them, then closed my robe and never looked down at them again.

When I told a few friends and loved ones about the private "funeral" I had for my breasts, each person was incredibly understanding and reassured me that it was a healthy thing to do. What a gift to share that experience and feel completely supported.

Below are some sentiments that breast cancer survivors found inspiring or touching during the treatment phase of their illness:

"That I was beautiful, that I was loved, and that they would always be there for me." --Kimberly B., age 55

"I became very depressed during treatment. I didn't want to talk to or see anyone. Most people stopped trying to reach me but one very good friend never gave up trying to reach me. He would write me letters and send me cards letting me know that he was thinking of me and praying for me. I found that very touching." --Isabel N., age 35

"They helped me count down the number of treatments both with chemo and radiation." --Karen S., age 49

"You're going to beat this, stay strong, we love you." --Deanna R., age 47

"One of my sisters would always tell me that I was going to beat the disease and it wasn't going to come back." --Anonymous, age 61

"I am just beginning and my cousin who has been through this said it was tough, but I can do it. Take care of myself and listen to my body." --Gwen C., age 49

"I met many people in the waiting area at chemo and radiation who reminded me that we had it very good!" --Sheryl R., age 42

"One friend told me that she had always thought that I was the strongest person she'd ever met, and that each day since my diagnosis I had continually proved her right." --Pink Warrior, age 55

What not to say (or at least be wary of)

As difficult as the treatment stage is for the woman with breast cancer, friends and family must contend with their own heartache. If you're watching a loved one undergo surgeries, radiation, or chemotherapy, you'll see someone who physically isn't herself, which can be unsettling. She may have lost a breast or two, be listless, or in the case of chemotherapy, not have her hair anymore and look ill. Her spirits may be down, which can make friends and family anxious. In addition, those closest to her might be questioning whether the treatment is working or not. When confronted with such a stressful situation, even the most well-intentioned loved ones can say things that we--the women fighting breast cancer--don't want to hear.

Below are comments breast cancer survivors found hurtful or wished someone hadn't said during treatment:

"Whenever anyone mentioned that someone they knew had died of cancer was very difficult for me to hear." --Isabel N., age 35

"Someone at work decided to tease me about my wig and yanked on the back of it so it slipped off my head to the back. I was so mad and annoyed at the meanness of this that I turned around and slapped the person really hard!" --Anonymous, age 61

"After hair loss, being told you have a 'good-shaped head' just seems like a consolation prize, it doesn't really make you feel better about being bald." --Valerie K., age 36

"Right after surgery time 1 (and I do mean right after, as in within the first 24 hours), my mom said, 'Well, now that they got it all, you can put this behind you and get on with your life.' Umm, right. Like I can immediately forget about this and get over it in 2 seconds?" --Anonymous, age 56

"My in-laws told me how I shouldn't have the procedure I had selected for breast cancer surgery and went on to tell me all the horrible things that could happen to me." --JZ, age 47

A word on hair...

A frequent comment people make to someone who's undergoing chemotherapy and lost her hair is, *"It's only hair, it'll grow back."* Oh-goodness-gracious-me-oh-my, please, please don't ever say that to anyone going through this. In the grand scheme of things, we know that losing our hair is just one of the many sacrifices we'll make to save our lives. We're not stupid; we know that getting out of this pickle is way more important than our hair. But make no mistake, it still sucks to lose it. Even though I knew it was coming, seeing my twenty inches of hair fall out in chunks was still shocking. Then my eyebrows and eyelashes fell away little by little and I felt like my whole face disappeared. Many days, mirrors were not my friend. The ironic thing is that even if you feel okay, you tend to look sick if you've lost every single hair on your entire body. No amount of makeup, nor skillful application, was going to make me look like myself, at least in my opinion. Can you see how *"It's only hair, it'll grow back"* sounds super insensitive and flippant, even if you don't mean it that way?

A better sentiment is a simple, *"I'm so sorry that this is happening."* And if your friend is upset, there's nothing wrong with the occasional, *"It stinks that you have to deal with this"* or an *"It's not fair."* Anything to validate how we're feeling is always appreciated.

Another thing to keep in mind: please don't complain about having a bad hair day around your friend. At least you have some!

One last piece of advice on hair: we'd rather you didn't tell us *"how much fun it's going to be to pick out a new wig, because you've always wanted long hair, red hair, blond hair, curly hair, straight hair, (fill in the blank) anyway."* Sure, I was curious over the years what it would be like to have a drastically different hairstyle and color, but when it came right down to it, I just wanted my own hair back.

Acts of kindness

In a way, this is when acts of kindness are most important. Of course someone feels vulnerable when they're first diagnosed, but the treatment phase is a completely different experience. Not only is a woman with breast cancer in the middle of her journey and facing all sorts of tangible fears, she's physically limited at times and needs help and encouragement. With breast cancer, you really do have to relinquish some control, because it's not exactly business as usual. After my double mastectomy and reconstruction, I wasn't allowed to lift or hold my 11 month-old baby for three weeks. As much as I wanted to, I couldn't. And three weeks seemed like an eternity.

During this phase, I was grateful for every bit of kindness shown me, whether it was a funny card, an encouraging word, a book I'd be interested in, or a gift certificate to one of my favorite restaurants. Every gesture, meaningful in its own way, made me smile and boosted my spirits for days.

Household

Here are some suggestions under the household category:

- Food is always appreciated, because even if we don't feel like it, we have to eat, as does our family. If you get the go-ahead from your friend, cook a meal that can be eaten right away and one that can be frozen.

- Offer to go grocery shopping for your friend. Better yet, pick up extras and prepare a meal at her house if she can't leave or doesn't feel like going out.

- Cook dinner regularly for your friend and invite her over to your place. I have a girlfriend who's a fabulous cook and puts a lot of love into each meal. She prepared food regularly for me during treatment, and not only was it nice to be pampered, I enjoyed the outings during the weeks I felt well.

- If it's holiday time or a special occasion (birthday, graduation, etc.), offer to make the celebratory meal or have her as a guest in your home. My Aunt Claudette is known for her tourtière (French pork pie) which is the main attraction at each Christmas dinner. Everyone in the family looks forward to this once-a-year treat. This past year, she was undergoing chemotherapy during the holidays. Using the family recipe, my sister Lorraine made all of Aunt Claudette's tourtière for her, a thoughtful gesture that meant the world to our very special aunt.

- Give a gift certificate to a favorite restaurant. Thoughtful friends did this for me during chemotherapy, and I was incredibly touched. Four mothers from my son's playgroup contributed to a very generous certificate, from which my family enjoyed several meals.

- Send a beautiful fruit basket or an edible arrangement. A girlfriend and her wonderful family sent an edible arrangement after I had my major surgery, and it was a fun and delicious pick-me-up.

- Offer to clean your friend's home for a few hours. This could include doing dishes, vacuuming, scrubbing bathrooms, laundry, taking recyclables away, and collecting garbage. If you don't live nearby, consider a gift certificate from a cleaning service—but please ask first, because some people would love this, others not so much.

- Mow/water lawns, weed gardens, rake leaves, or shovel snow.

- If your friend has small children, offer to take them to get their hair cut or other appointments. Perhaps you could also help with shopping for school projects, books, clothes, or birthday presents. Take them on fun outings to the movies or playdates. Children may be frightened during this time and need some semblance of normalcy doing regular kids' stuff.

- Helping with pets is appreciated, too, whether it's to take them to an appointment or out for a walk.

- Offer to run errands.

Below are "household" acts of kindness breast cancer survivors found helpful and thoughtful:

"Friends helped during chemo when I was too weak to do daily mundane tasks, including delivering groceries to sweeping my floors and taking out my trash." --Deena B., age 41

"My best friend arranged dinners for our family for two weeks starting the Friday I came home from the hospital. My Godmother flew in from Washington, D.C. and stayed with us for ten days...doing laundry, driving, changing bandages, charting drains!!!!" --JZ, age 47

"It's frustrating to go from being independent to suddenly unable to complete household chores, seeing your garden wither and die, your pets diverge from their routine, being unable to walk two blocks to a local restaurant. From surgery to radiation to chemotherapy these helps on the 'bad' days were invaluable." --Valerie K., age 36

"My neighbor was great about checking on my children and keeping my 11 year-old active. My 18 year-old daughter would take my son to the bus stop every morning during my radiation as you had to be there by 8am." --Anonymous

"We had friends from our church give us gift

certificates to 'Entrée Express,' a local company that picks up food from a number of different restaurants around town and delivers them to your door. That was extremely generous and made me cry." --Anonymous, age 40

"Two people I didn't know helped with lodging so I wasn't sleeping in my car or on hospital couches at the cancer center." --Anonymous, age 56

"During my chemo treatment, one of my co-workers got us a takeout lunch and brought it over to my house on the weekend." --Anonymous, age 61

"Several people provided meals for me and my family while I was going through chemo. It was great because they could just be warmed up or thrown into the crock pot. It was a tremendous help." --Barb C., age 52

"I was diagnosed with breast cancer in my early 30s. My girls were 12 and 14 at the time, so any help with them was greatly appreciated." --Jan S., age 68

"My son (then 18) helped with laundry, dishes, and shopping when he was home from school. He had started college 200 miles away just a month before my diagnosis." --Anonymous, age 60

"During my four rounds of chemo, my live-in boyfriend was my caregiver. He did all the shopping, cooking, and everything else that I was too sick to do. His help was so meaningful to me." --Anonymous, age 42

"My mother came to stay for a few days with me (I am a single mom) when I got home from the hospital. I remember waking and knowing she was there and feeling so safe. My oldest daughter and her fiancé would come clean the house every weekend for me when I was having chemo. It was wonderful. My youngest daughter's friend, who was rooming with us at the time, went and got me food when I was all alone and had worked all day." --Anonymous, age 61

"During the time after my lumpectomy, I was unable to provide my family with the "normal" level of support. I have a very supportive husband and a circle of friends who helped by tending to the everyday needs such as carpooling for the kids and meals for the family. It was rewarding to see that there were so many people who cared so much." --Michele R., age 46

"My husband did his best at helping with meals. I had frozen meals in the freezer, although he was good at bringing in meals. This was a big deal for him because cooking is not his thing. He did all of the cleaning and took care of the laundry. My diagnosis and surgery happened so fast that we hardly had time to turn around, let alone think about it and then the radiation was immediately after the surgery. We felt as though we were on a merry-go-round and then all of a sudden it stopped. My husband was there for me every step of the way." --Dorothy G., age 69

"My fiancé, now my husband, was my caregiver during treatment. He was with me through my diagnosis and all following procedures. His way of taking care of our

home and pets, my garden, and making meals was very good, but not done as I would have done them, and this helped me to feel that I was needed, that I had to get through this so that I would be able to resume taking care of the things I love most. He doted on me through my recovery from each surgery and from my treatment. He also communicated an expectation that I would soon be back on my feet and doing well. This helped me to keep that goal in mind." --Kimberly B., age 55

"As a mom/wife, it's hard to give up and accept help during chemo. My family and friends were invaluable." --Sheryl R., age 42

Logistics

Here are some suggestions under the logistics category:

- Offer to do research on any aspect of your friend's illness or treatment, or anything else that interests her, such as nutrition or alternative medicine (i.e., acupuncture, Reiki, visualization).

- Offer to copy, organize, or file the mountain of medical and insurance paperwork your friend will be buried under. Anyone battling cancer will tell you that keeping all of it straight can feel like a full-time job.

- Offer to be the point person/disseminator of information about your friend (as early in this process as possible). If your friend is amenable, you could be the key communicator to other friends and acquaintances, the one to say, "She's not having a good day, but will look forward to hearing from you tomorrow" or "I know she'd love to go shopping one day this week" or "She's had a rough week and would appreciate an encouraging email." In addition, there are websites to keep everyone apprised of how she's doing, and perhaps you could be in charge of updating it weekly. Or go to www.lotsahelpinghands.com and get started on coordinating efforts among a group of you. The idea behind this website is "free, private, web-based communities for organizing friends, family, and colleagues during times of need. Easily coordinate activities and manage volunteers with an intuitive group calendar."

- Drive your friend to some of her medical appointments, radiation and/or chemotherapy sessions. If you're able (and she wants you to), offer to sit with her during treatment.

- Offer to be with her during meetings with doctors and take notes.

- If you work with your friend, offer to help with tasks at the office.

Below are "logistical" acts of kindness breast cancer survivors found helpful and thoughtful:

"I worked the entire time. My staff went overboard with trying to assist. My physicians (most of whom are friends) also called everyday to see if I had any questions." --Karen S., age 49

"I had a very dear and steadfast friend who took charge of my life and did everything I needed, which included helping my son (and his wife) understand what was going on. I didn't have to do anything but concentrate on getting better. My colleagues at work always let me know that they would cover until I was able to get back in gear." --Anonymous, age 66

"During treatment for surgery and first chemo session, my 'second mom' attended meaningful/tough surgical appointments." --Deena B., age 41

"My mother in-law quite often sat with me during chemo when my husband was unable to." --Barb C., age 52

Events and Activities

The following are some suggestions under the "events and activities" category:

- Your friend may be feeling cooped up and stir-crazy, in which case a change of scenery can be fabulous medicine. Take her on a day trip if she's up for it, and if not, a quick drive for pleasure is nice, too. Two of my closest friends took me out to lunch or dinner to different restaurants whenever they were in town. Their company, as well as an enjoyable outing in a new environment, always lifted my spirits.

- Get tickets for a special event, such as a concert, comedy club, or the theater, to name just a few. Whether it's music, laughter, or drama, what a fun way to get her mind off the seriousness of her situation.

- Do a cancer walk/marathon in your friend's name. My husband's family did this for me back in Montreal, and when I saw the pictures, it took my breath away. There they were, wearing t-shirts with my name across their chests and walking with others who had been touched by breast cancer. I didn't know about the event ahead of time and was so moved by their gesture. To this day, those photos make my eyes well with tears of appreciation.

- Some friends may love this idea or hate it, depending on how they want to remember (or not remember) their breast cancer experience: offer to document her journey in photos or video. Later on, she may not want to see herself when she was most vulnerable; on the other hand, she might be grateful to have it all on record. I carry a picture of myself right after one of my chemo treatments, bald and sick and curled up in the fetal position. When I'm having a challenging day, I grab it out of my son's diaper bag. What a wonderful reminder of where I've been and how far I've come.

- If your friend will be having chemotherapy treatments and losing her hair, going with her ahead of time to select a wig (or hats or scarves) is one of the most thoughtful things you can do. My best friend lives over two thousand miles away but sent me an American Express gift card to buy a wig. What an incredibly generous gesture. When I lost my hair, that wig made me feel normal again, and when I wore it in public, no one gave me the "you-poor-thing-you-have-cancer" look. What a gift.

- Offer to take your friend to a salon or spa and treat her to a massage, manicure, or pedicure. Pampering is a wonderful antithesis to a rigorous treatment program, and these services are great pick-me-ups when your friend is feeling "blah."

Here are what some survivors said were wonderful events or activities during treatment:

"My husband took me on several day motorcycle trips into the mountains. We would ride down the road, through pine forests, breathing in the clean air. I remember the tears running down my face as we rode along...my body was still intact, I was awaiting surgery...I thought I was going to die. The memories of that trip stayed with me through surgery and initial treatment. I could close my eyes and remember the beautiful views and the feeling of the

cool wind…and would try to visualize that during the roughest parts of my initial journey." --Kimberly B., age 55

"My hairdresser went with me to look for wigs, as did a great friend of mine (patiently). Some of my friends attended the Revlon Run/Walk with me one month post chemo." --Deena B., age 41

"Wigs are so expensive! I didn't know where to go to get one. And wasn't sure that I could even afford one. My wonderful friend surprised me with one, right in the nick of time. That was an incredible act of kindness I will never forget." --Isabel, age 35

"My sister and oldest daughter went with me to get my wig before I started treatment. It was pretty disastrous. My daughter ended up having to go outside because she was crying. My brother would take me for lunches and drives down the coast because he knew I loved the beach. And my brother took me to many rock & roll concerts through my treatment because he knew that was my favorite thing ever!! I felt so nervous in my wig, like any second it would accidentally get ripped off and I would be standing there bald!!" --Anonymous, age 61

"My staff and family signed up for every breast cancer walk. Together we raised money to try and help others. I purchased and donated my wigs." --Karen S., age 49

"Just before my hair fell out, my friends at work had

a 'hat party' for me...I hated my wig and wore hats or caps most of the time...it was very fun and inspiring! When my hair came back and I didn't need all of my hats, I had an auction for them and raised more than $200 for the cancer society." --Anonymous, age 66

"My co-workers said prayers for me and we started having 'Pink Tuesdays' where everyone was encouraged to wear something pink in honor of the three of us who were all in different stages of the treatment/recovery process." --Anonymous

"My husband took me to pick out a wig before I started chemo. My sister in-law did a 3-day walk shortly after my treatments ended." --Anonymous, age 60

"When I was able to get out, my stepdad would take me for a drive to see the outdoors instead of staring at the walls of my room." --Deanna R., age 47

"A team was created in my honor called 'Shakin' it for Sheryl' and I walked with my team a few days after chemo. I wore a wig and had many friends who sent me scarves, catalogs. My husband took me for rides, held my hand, and told me that everything would be okay. And you know what? It was." --Sheryl R., age 42

"Just to get out and drive (no place in particular) with a friend was time to keep from worrying." --Anonymous, age 66

"My sister going with me to get scarves and helping

me tie them. Getting a wig, which I haven't worn yet but it's fun to put it on and know that I have it. Getting new bras and a new prosthetic right breast. The women there are so loving and understanding. We tried many breasts to get the fit and to match the left. Love the new breast and they always hug me when I go to pick up something—first it was drain pouches, then the bras, then the new breast."
--Gwen C., age 49

"I picked up the 'Making Strides' brochure in the doctor's office and my granddaughter ran with the idea and we got a team together. 'Walkers for Knockers' sent out emails for donations and had a team that walked on the 22nd. This all happened as I was diagnosed, had surgery, under-went radiation, and recovery, a merry-go-round. I was very proud of my family and friends." --Dorothy G., age 69

"Once again, I have to say that any kind of activities that brought about a sense of normalcy were by far the most meaningful to me. Though I never attended a walk in my honor, I did attend the Komen Walk with my future daughter in-law and very close friend. This was a fantastic day because all survivors were honored, and to see the large number of them gave me great hope and pride for my achievements." --Pink Warrior, age 55

Gifts

The possibilities seem endless for gifts, and each can be as unique as your friendship. You have lots of room to be creative according to your friend's tastes, interests, sense of humor, your history together, and so on. No list is exhaustive, but here are some ideas:

- Assemble a gift basket tailored to your friend. Two of my girlfriends from graduate school sent me an incredible care package while I was going through chemotherapy. What made the gift so special was that they put a great deal of thought into it and took the time to research what I might find useful while having treatments. Among some of the items in their goody box was the softest robe I've ever felt (because skin becomes very sensitive); luxurious hand/body cream and lip balm (for the dry skin and chapped lips that come with chemo); ginger drops and special tea from Africa (to help with nausea); and a calming cd (because chemo can frazzle your nerves). They blew me away, they really did. Truthfully, I get choked up each time I think about the kind spirit in which the gift was given.

- If your friend is undergoing chemotherapy, the above-mentioned items are perfect for a care package. Another suggestion is a warm, soft blanket. Oftentimes, infusion rooms are chilly. At the cancer center where I received treatments, infusions are done in the basement. That alone hints that a cozy blanket would come in handy! An alternative to a blanket is a wraparound that will keep your friend comfortable during her drips. I was incredibly touched when a friend's thoughtful mother gave me one. Similarly, a soft knit hat is another wonderful gift. When you're bald, you are reminded all the time of how much warmth your hair used to provide, as well as protection. Bumping your bald head hurts like hell. A soft hat provides a buffer from cold, and if you're clumsy like me, from objects that get in your way.

- Along that same line, if your friend is having radiation, one of the primary side effects is tender, swollen skin. Anything that eases her discomfort will be appreciated. Suggestions for a care package include very soft cotton tank tops, t-shirts, or camisoles (because wearing a bra is often out of the question), ibuprophen for swelling, aloe vera to cool and moisturize, and sunscreen for extra protection once the treatments are over.

- Oftentimes when you're undergoing cancer treatments, your skin takes on a strange color and its texture may change completely. A very dear friend knew that this was one of my side effects from the chemotherapy drugs and bought me a certificate for a wonderful skincare line. We couldn't do anything about my ashy color, because that would take time. But the texture of my skin improved a great deal, and make-up didn't look so funky. Call it a girlie moment, but I was thankful that she recognized my desire to look more like my old self.

- If your friend enjoys reading, now's a great time to give her books and magazine subscriptions.

There's a lot of downtime during this stage of her illness, whether it's because she's waiting for doctors' appointments, having a treatment, spending time in the hospital, or just nesting at home. (A note of caution: don't feel like you need to give her self-help or "How to Beat Cancer in 5 Easy Steps" titles. I think a little escapism is appreciated, although you know your friend best). My oldest, dearest friend— who just happens to be a literacy specialist— sent me many books during my illness, all carefully chosen according to what seemed most inspirational and uplifting at the time. Each book was a treasure and a reminder of our history and love of reading.

- A unique piece of jewelry can be a lovely, highly personal token of your love for your friend. During my illness, my sister gave me a necklace with an inscription by Ralph Waldo Emerson: *"What lies behind us and what lies before us are tiny matters compared to what lies within us."* A heartfelt sentiment on beautiful jewelry from someone I adore? A homerun.

- When you're fighting breast cancer, there are days when you don't feel like talking to anyone yet still want to keep in touch and stay connected. During those times, it's handy to have an assortment of blank cards and stationery, as well as a good pen and a roll of stamps. A friend gave me this present, and I loved the practicality and thoughtfulness of it. She also included a box of thank you cards knowing that I had notes to send out for gifts I had received.

- Most people would agree that music can be therapeutic. Why not compile a list of songs and music she'd like? A very generous gift is an Ipod with songs you download for her (or if she already has one, ask to borrow it so that you can add to her playlist). Good tunes could lift her spirits or calm her, depending on what she needs. I always saw several patients listening to Ipods during their chemo drips, and they usually looked relaxed and content. If technology isn't your forte or a new Ipod isn't within your budget, a carefully-chosen cd is just as thoughtful.

- Craftsmanship isn't where my talents lie, so I'm always awestruck by those who can create beautiful things with their hands. If you are gifted (sorry for the pun) in this way, your friend will treasure something you've made just for her, whether it's pottery, a painting, or a warm shawl. One of my dearest friend's mother made lovely, needlepoint tea cloths for me, and another thoughtful friend who carves exquisite, decorative wooden boxes gave me one during treatment. I admire each of these cherished possessions frequently and feel so fortunate to have them.

- One of my all-time favorite gifts was a Breville juicer from my sister, brother in-law, and nephew. I used it often when I was pregnant, breastfeeding, and during all phases of my breast cancer. I swear, you feel healthier immediately after having a juice made of spinach, kale, carrots, apples, peppers, tomatoes, etc. There were times during chemotherapy when most foods didn't appeal to me, but I could always manage to drink a large glass of homemade juice, even if I had to plug my nose. Good, sturdy juicers tend to be expensive, so it might be an appropriate group gift. You could also include a juicing recipe book, or compile recipes from the internet, and perhaps get her started with a grocery bag full of super cancer-fighting foods (see chapter 4). Helping your friend get back on the path to wellness is a fantastic way to show her that you care.

- If you feel strongly that an organization is doing good work for breast cancer research, providing services such as mammograms to uninsured women, or donating wigs to ladies in need (the list goes on and on), consider making a donation in honor of your friend. Unfortunately, the breast cancer community is growing, and helping even just one person will feel great. For suggestions, please refer to Appendices B, C, and D.

- The old adage "laughter is the best medicine"

exists for a reason. Studies have shown that laughter boosts the immune system, which is exactly what your friend needs right now. Rent or buy funny TV shows and movies on DVD and offer to watch them with her. She'll enjoy the escape that your visit and the entertainment provide. For a list of the top comedies from the past few decades, please refer to Appendix E.

- Flowers and plants are classic and always appreciated. You probably have an idea of which flower variety your friend likes best, as well as whether she has a green thumb or not. If taking care of plants isn't her thing, be sure to buy something that's hearty and requires little maintenance. I think flowers are cheerier and brighten any space, but they also don't last.

- As mentioned before, there's a lot of downtime during the treatment stage of breast cancer. Solitary activities such as working on crossword puzzles (or jigsaw puzzles, word games, brain teasers, or trivia) can be relaxing and enjoyable distractions. Some of these are electronic, some are more old-school, but either way, a collection based on your friend's interests will be a hit.

- Finally, never underestimate the power of words. The cards, letters, little notes, emails, and phone calls keep us going. They take little time, but forever stay with someone battling breast cancer. As Michele R., 46, explains,

"Cards and letters were welcome at any stage of my illness. They brightened my day and I am sure the well wishes and support impacted my mental state in a positive capacity." One of my closest friends sent me a card every single week after my diagnosis and during treatment. She knew the dates of all my chemo sessions and still sends uplifting and life-affirming notes marking special anniversaries related to my breast cancer journey. What treasures they are!

Below are wonderful gifts some survivors said they received during treatment:

"My co-workers sent me care packages while I was out on medical leave. The care packages included flowers, movies, magazines, cookies, and most importantly... encouraging get well cards. All these items reminded me that I was not alone and had people around me who were praying for me." --Isabel N., age 35

"My brother gave me a certificate for a massage, which was great because I had never had one. My friend at work gave me a lovely mug and some tea because she knew I loved to sit and relax with a hot cup of tea. I received many flower gifts throughout my treatment, and I went to several musical concerts." --Anonymous, age 61

"When I arrived home after my surgery, I had received a number of plants and well-wishes. The thing that meant the most to me was a bouquet of beautiful pink roses. This reminded me of the strength that it had taken to

get through this point. Each anniversary since I have purchased for myself a bouquet of pink roses to remind me of that strength." --Pink Warrior, age 55

"When my brother heard I had cancer and losing my hair, he shaved his head. When I saw the picture I was so touched I showed it to everyone. I was a proud little sister. He also organized a team and participated in a breast cancer walk in Memphis in October, 2009. Many of my co-workers donated to the cause. It was wonderful to get all of the support." --Deanna R., age 47

"I received anonymous donations of subscriptions to Cure and other magazines." --Kimberly B., age 55

"My kitchen was filled with flowers and gifts—just amazing." --Sheryl R., age 42

"Donations made by friends to the Revlon Run/Walk 2010." --Deena B., age 41

"One friend brought me flowers after my surgery. Really hurtful that most kept their distance, probably because they didn't know what to say." --Gail N., age 57

"Each gift meant so much to me. They arrived at various times in my treatment…each thing was a blessing, not because of what it was, but because of the love that it was given with. When I did not want to fight, I was reminded by all that was provided for me that others were there to fight with me, that I was not alone." --Kimberly B., age 55

Below are "other" acts of kindness survivors described as meaningful during the treatment phase of their illness:

"Prayers by innumerable people. I also received a prayer shawl." --Jan K., age 59

"My family and friends did so much for me during my treatment, too many to list. But I have to say that having their company and support is what I appreciated the most." --Isabel N., age 35

"When I would enter stores they would open a line just for me. People would just come up to me who had been through cancer/chemo and ask what type I had. Found that people would hold open doors for me or offer up their chair. Most support came from my husband. After each chemo he would spend it with me on the bathroom floor. Never left my side while I was ill. Together we experienced every-thing. I think it was harder on him than me." --Karen S., age 49

"The visits, people taking time to stop by and say hi and encourage. I am in the middle so I am sure there will be many more." --Gwen C., age 49

"A lifelong friend flew across the country to be with me for some of my more painful and difficult treatments. My daughter in-law sat at the hospital with me, massaging my feet. My mother spent the first night after my surgery sleeping in a chair by my hospital bed. I was given a standing ovation by the entire student body of the campus

that I worked at." Kimberly B., age 55

"Throughout my illness, diagnosed 7/15/09, chemo, surgery, radiation, surgery again, side effects, complications, and more surgery to come, I have had tremendous support and kindness from family, friends, and co-workers. I still have a long ways to go and the kindness of others during this time really helps me stay on track and say, 'I am going to beat this'." --Deanna R., age 47

"Reinforced how wonderful people can be. The little acts of kindness mean the most." --Karen S., age 49

Chapter 3

Recovery

What your friend may be thinking

There's no question, reaching the remission phase of breast cancer is a hard-fought victory and should be celebrated. But this "re-entry" stage is a strange time for everyone. Your friend is likely to be ambivalent; she's happy to be done with the treatment phase of her journey but may not be ready to blow the party horns just yet. For perhaps as much as a year (maybe more), this has been a full-time job and the focus of all her attention and energy. She got used to the new routine and felt safe being looked after closely by a team of trusted medical professionals. She's been in survival mode and fighting like hell, and now she can actually step back and take a breath. In a way, time stands still during treatment because she's in the "getting better" zone, but it catches up during recovery. Suddenly there are more hours to reflect on what's just taken place.

Don't be surprised if now's her time to mourn. Recognize that she may be grieving part of a breast, an entire breast, or both breasts; her hair and possibly her fertility if she underwent chemotherapy; some aspect of her sexuality; a sense of fairness or vision of how her life would unfold; time lost with loved ones or friends; or worse yet, people she thought she could count on who never reached out. I admit, I allowed myself to grieve all of these things.

As content as I was with my baby boy, I also felt sad that I'd never get pregnant again because of chemotherapy. Also, some measure of regret, and certainly guilt, set in when I thought about the time I had lost with my son, about nine precious months, because of not feeling well. It was a formative block of time in his development that I knew we'd never get back. I mourned friendships that came up short. However, with some time and distance, I realized that not everyone is wired to reach out in a crisis. What appears to be indifference is not necessarily intentional. I took a little time to grieve my idyllic picture of how things shoulda-woulda-coulda been. Experiencing the hurt and unpleasantness was an important part of my personal healing process.

Even the best attempts at getting back to "normal" may be undermined if fearful thoughts creep in, though. Survivors often mention things that trigger concerns about recurrence, such as being run down and tired, not feeling well, or having an ache in their bones or side. Anniversaries of diagnosis, treatment, end of treatment, or doctors' appointments can be joyous occasions ("I kicked cancer's ass!") or may set off anxiety alarms ("Are there cancer cells still lingering? Will it come back? Am I really okay?")

Also, hearing about cancer returning in others is tough. As a survivor, you belong to a special group and your heart goes out to fellow breast cancer warriors who must face the beast again. At the same time, it's a reminder that it could happen to you, too. In just the past few months, I've heard about several women having recurrences in their bones and liver. I admit, it's made me take pause each time I feel a little sore here and there. I think that's something survivors must learn to live with. Again, patience and understanding are genuine gifts you can offer your friend now.

Understanding her medical maintenance

Phew! Your friend has made it through the roughest part of her treatment, whether she underwent surgery, radiation, or chemotherapy. But her journey is far from over, because moving forward, her medical maintenance will be a critical factor in staying well. During the next few years, she'll continue to see her doctors often, and someone will be keeping a close eye on her for the rest of her life. Note that the timelines discussed below are general guides. Your friend may have a slightly different schedule.

- **Oncologist**: particularly if your friend has had

chemotherapy, her oncologist will be the primary doctor in charge of her care for the first several years after treatment. Typically this means that she'll see him/her every three months for blood work during the first three years, twice a year for the next two years, and annually after the fifth year. The work up consists of your friend's blood count (white and red blood cell counts, platelet volume, etc.); protein markers that when elevated suggest a possible tumor (these tests include CEA, CA 15-3, and CA 27-29) [25]; and liver blood tests that may be able to detect an early metastasis. The oncologist may also order blood work to check hormone levels. This assesses whether your friend is menopausal or not, the results of which will guide treatment strategies (discussed in this chapter, below). In addition, weight, temperature, and blood pressure are taken during these appointments. Finally, the oncologist will ask about overall health, any residual symptoms or side effects that your friend may be experiencing (such as lymphedema or fatigue), and discuss any concerns that she may have.

- **Breast surgeon or specialist**: for the first few years after treatment, your friend will likely see this specialist twice each year for thorough breast exams, even if she's had reconstruction. During this examination, the doctor is looking and feeling for any signs that the cancer has returned locally, meaning in the breasts and chest, as well as nearby lymph nodes in the neck/collarbone area and under the arms. After the three-year mark, this specialist is seen annually for the rest of your friend's life.

- **Gynecologist**: because there is a link between breast cancer and other female cancers, it's recommended that your friend see her gynecologist twice a year, at least for the first few years after completion of her treatment. Appointments typically include transvaginal ultrasounds, pelvic exams, and pap smears. Also, a gynecologist is critical in assessing and treating issues related to hormones, including fertility, sexual dysfunction, and menopausal symptoms.

- **Primary care physician**: annual check-ups are important because your friend's oncologist is in the business of cancer care and management, not other health problems independent of cancer that might pop up. Blood work to keep an eye on cholesterol levels and thyroid function, for example, should be routine, as well as updating flu and tetanus shots, etc.

Other tests

In addition to the tests mentioned above, your friend will also need the following after treatment:

- **Mammogram**: if your friend had breast-conserving surgery (lumpectomy), her doctor will likely recommend that she have a mammogram twice a year for the first few years, then once a year after that. However, if she's had a bilateral mastectomy, she'll never need a mammogram again.

- **CT, PET, and bone scans, MRI** (maybe): if your friend's tumor markers are elevated, her physical examination suggests a recurrence, or her doctor is cautious, some of these tests may be ordered.

Hormone therapy

As discussed in chapter one, most breast cancer tumors need estrogen and/or progesterone to grow. Hormonal therapy reduces the risk of breast cancer after treatment (adjuvant therapy) by lowering estrogen levels or blocking the estrogen receptors on breast cancer cells. In doing this, estrogen cannot adhere to the surface of the breast cancer cell. This is critical because if allowed to bind to the cancer cell, estrogen triggers DNA that tells the cancer cell to divide (and grow). [26] Hormone therapy is not effective for tumors that are estrogen and progesterone negative.

The most widely-used anti-estrogen drug is tamoxifen, which can be used to reduce the risk of cancer returning, lower the chance of developing breast cancer in high risk women, or treat those with metastatic breast cancer. Tamoxifen is dispensed in pill form and can be taken daily for five years in pre-menopausal women. Side effects often include hot flashes, vaginal dryness, and mood swings. Tamoxifen also increases the risk of uterine cancer, which makes pelvic exams during this time particularly important.

After two to three years of tamoxifen, or if a woman is post-menopausal, she will be prescribed an aromatase inhibitor. These drugs block aromatase, which is an enzyme that makes small amounts of estrogen in post-menopausal women. [27] Also taken in pill form, they generally have fewer side effects than tamoxifen. However, thinning bones are a concern for those on aromatase inhibitors, so bone density tests should be done periodically. As with tamoxifen, some aromatase inhibitors may be used for early or advanced breast cancer.

Targeted therapies

As discussed in chapter 2, trastuzumab (herceptin) is administered for one year. The goal of this adjuvant therapy is to lower the risk of recurrence. However, it has also been known to reduce the size of other HER2-neu positive tumors that may return after chemotherapy. If breast cancer spreads to other organs, trastuzumab or another HER2-neu suppressing drug, lapatinib (commonly known as tykerb), may be used as a systemic treatment. [28]

How to help her: what to say, what not to say, and acts of kindness

Suggestions on what to say

Loved ones walk a tightrope between not forgetting what the breast cancer survivor has been through and reminding her of it when she'd rather not remember. During treatment, she is singularly focused on getting better, and the cancer talk is normal. But now the worst part of the storm has passed. Just because your friend wanted to discuss her medical crisis then doesn't necessarily mean that she wants to be asked about it all the time now.

Soon after she's done with treatment, by all means, show your enthusiasm and be sure to express how proud you are of her strength, courage, and resiliency. She just went to war and came out on the other side, which is a hell of an accomplishment. Comments that I appreciated during recovery were, *"I hope you feel as great as you look!"* and *"Take it one day at a time."* The first I was thankful for because it was a compliment and yet acknowledged that it would take time to physically feel like my old self. The second I liked because it was measured and calming, as if to say, *"Take a deep breath and re-boot. Be patient and kind to yourself."*

Below are comments other breast cancer survivors were happy to hear during recovery:

"My co-workers made a big deal about me completing treatment. They got a cake and praised me." --Isabel N., age 35

"My sister always tells me how inspiring and strong I am. She tells me I am a survivor and doesn't know how I managed to work everyday and still battle cancer twice. She also tells me how good I look and how pretty I am.

(Ha!)" --Anonymous, age 61

"We knew you could beat this!" --Anonymous, age 52

"They continue to encourage me, support me...to tell me that I am loved and needed in their lives." --Kimberly B., age 55

"Constantly being told that they knew I could beat it, as did I." --Sheryl R., age 42

"I have had several friends and women who were recently diagnosed with breast cancer tell me I have been an inspiration and they admired the strength I showed during the radiation. When co-workers/volunteers are diagnosed, they now come to me for support." --Anonymous

As time goes on, I think the best rule of thumb is to be straightforward and ask your friend if she wants to talk about anything cancer-related. Some survivors need and want to, others don't. Some need to vent and analyze, others never want to hear the words breast cancer again. No matter what her coping strategy, be earnest that you're there for her in whichever way is most helpful.

This is also a good opportunity to flip your emotional intelligence switch on and focus your undivided attention to mannerisms, tone of voice, eye contact, posture, and body language to assess what your friend wants. I know one survivor who often seems eager to talk about her breast cancer experiences, past and present, then hits a wall. Her posture shifts, eyes wander, and she hurries her speech, all signs that she wants to move on to something else. Of course, cancer doesn't encapsulate all that any survivor is, so certainly feel free to talk about other things!

What not to say (or at least be wary of)

One erroneous assumption people make is that once a survivor's physical wounds have healed, her spirit has, too. This is a long journey, one that the survivor sets out on at her own pace. Although well-intentioned, the *"Now you can get on with your life," "Now that it's all over,"* and *"You must be happy to have that behind you!"* disregard the difficult road we have traveled, the uncertainty of our new "normal," and the fear we have for the future. It's better to simply acknowledge that she is a strong, powerful warrior.

Something else that breast cancer survivors want you to know: be mindful of the way you ask, *"How are you?"* If you say it with pity in your voice, squint your eyes, and tilt your head a little, it looks and feels patronizing. We welcome compassion, but anything that makes us feel pathetic or like a victim leaves us cold. Also, *"How are you?"* is probably too broad right now. It's better to be specific: *"How is your appetite these days?"* or *"Are you sleeping well?"* or *"Will you be resuming your full work schedule?"* or *"Have you been going to your book club meetings?"*

If you're in the camp that believes you should

never censor yourself around a friend, I have to disagree. We don't need to be warned about the horrific side effects of this drug or that drug (we already know, and besides, that's what our doctors are for), and we don't want to hear about botched boob jobs, statistics, people who have had a recurrence, your second cousin who just died of breast cancer, or anything else that brings negative energy into our orbit. Exercise restraint, and if you have to ask if information is kind or not, it probably isn't.

Below are comments survivors found hurtful during recovery:

"Lots of people have commented to me how my hair is not the same as it used to be and how thin it is and how it has lost its body. Also they will comment on how my breasts don't match in size or how I look lopsided. I have many effects that chemo left me with and sometimes they really get me down and no one ever remembers this and I constantly have to remind them. I was telling one of my friends how worried I was about getting cancer again and she said something like, 'Well, a lot of people these days live 10 years more after having cancer.' Gee, I only have ten years left then, I felt." --Anonymous, age 61

"Oh, yes…grrrr. My supervisor at my job made the statement, 'Now that this is all over…' I burst into tears and told her how much I wished it was all over…that I had to carry with me the possibility of recurrence and eventually dying from this…I felt it was a statement made of ignorance and shallowness…it was very painful…I cried on

and off for days...it still hurts two years later...I eventually quit the job because of her lack of compassion." Kimberly B., age 55

"There is the presumption that you recover immediately, as soon as the physical recovery is over and that the psychic recovery should happen as fast." --Anonymous, age 56

"The thing people don't get is how long it takes to recover emotionally. You think about it everyday. It takes a really long time to have days where thoughts about breast cancer aren't at least a fleeting thought sometime during the day. I am allowed to be upset, pissed off, grieve, worry, be sad, cry...far longer than the first several days after being diagnosed. Don't tell me stress will make it worse, bad attitude will make it worse, and I need to smile and be happy because otherwise I will increase the odds of the cancer returning. First, there is no medical evidence that stress, attitude, etc., causes this, and second of all, telling me this twists it so that recurrence would be my fault. Third, this discounts the emotional side of a serious disease." --Anonymous, age 56

Acts of kindness

During the diagnosis and treatment phases of breast cancer, a woman is in crisis management mode. Her primary focus is on getting well, which requires a great deal of time. There are many opportunities for friends and loved ones to step in and help with home, work, and family, as well as offer emotional support.

Recovery

Although the pace of cancer management slows considerably during recovery, there are still plenty of ways to show kindness.

Many of the acts of kindness and gift ideas from chapters one and two are appropriate now. My personal favorites during recovery have been cards of support and encouragement, uplifting messages marking important anniversaries and milestones, and articles on the latest breast cancer news and research. I've also been touched by friends' and relatives' participation in breast cancer events (such as walks) and contributions to charities that will benefit other sister warriors.

You know your friend best, so trust that you can extend kindness in ways that are meaningful to her. My favorites might not be someone else's. Still, I think continued communication--letting her know how proud you are of her, for example--is one of the most thoughtful acts.

An important point to make is that even if you haven't been available for much of the diagnosis and treatment phases of your friend's illness, you have not missed the chance to reach out to her. Know that it's never too late to show you care!

Below are acts of kindness survivors indicated they found meaningful during recovery:

"Events and activities that made me feel normal...that life would go on." --Jan S., age 68

"A lot of laughter and education from friends who had already gone through breast cancer. Knowledge is power and laughter is the world's best medicine!" --Deena B., age 41

"Just for people to hug you and tell you how great you look." --Anonymous, age 66

"The Yahoo breast cancer support group has been invaluable to me in my recovery, getting through treatment, as well as the other side of cancer and dealing with what's next." --Jan K., age 59

"Just people caring…it amazed me that the people I worked with cared so much outside of work. My family, my friends, our kids and my husband were amazing." --Sheryl R., age 42

"I was diagnosed the day after my 50th birthday. On the 5th anniversary of my survival, I was lucky to celebrate both occasions surrounded by many friends and family members. Each one of my birthday gifts was pink and included a pink ribbon on it. I think everyone should celebrate their 'survival' days as they would any birthday, as it is truly a new beginning each year that we are given." --Pink Warrior, age 55

Body image and sexuality

Most survivors could write a book (or at least a pamphlet) on the effect breast cancer has had on their body image and sexuality. For many of us, each takes a hit.

Whether we're cognizant of it or not, we're bombarded with images in the media that promote and idealize a voluptuous female standard. The cultural expectation is that a "womanly" body type = beautiful = sexually robust = fertile = worthy. This standard contributes to the difficulty many women experience when coping with loss and accepting a new appearance, as well as feeling sexually vibrant.

Sexuality is private, and as one survivor said, *"I don't think that there is anything a friend can do to help in this area."* Still, women living with breast cancer in the treatment or remission phases want you to know that there is more at stake than just getting well. Many have lingering issues that cut deeper than any scalpel ever could (names omitted to protect privacy):

"I struggled and continue to struggle with accepting the way I look now. I feel very unattractive, and therefore would rather not be intimate with my partner. I am also heartbroken about the fact that I may not be able to have a child."

"I was sad to learn chemotherapy would force menopause, but fortunately my attitude is that when I am healthy and with the right person I can always adopt."

"I lost half of my breast. My husband was wonderful reminding me daily that he loves me, not my breast. I do still to this day, 3 years later, feel uncomfortable at times but I remind myself that I am alive..."

"You are definitely self-conscious about your body after losing a portion of your body to this disease but my husband reminded me that my eyes and smile have not changed. He is incredible."

"The feeling of being mutilated was strong."

"My sexuality has been significantly affected by the surgery and the treatment. I just can't physically respond as I used to...sex feels very mechanical, takes planning... nothing spontaneous about it anymore. Although I have almost completed reconstruction, my new breasts are just for looks. I see the scars every morning and night, and they are lifeless lumps. I look great in my clothes, marvelous cleavage, even have had nipples recreated and tattooed, but I am dead from the waist up...and almost dead from the waist down. Then there is the weight gain...not too bad, but it makes me feel old and frumpy and not so good about my appearance. My husband and family feel that I look better than I have in a long time, so maybe it looks okay from the outside, but does not feel okay from the inside."

Although you may not be able to help with sexuality issues, reminding your friend that she's beautiful is always kind. And remember, if she has the courage to discuss something so personal, be ready with an open heart and mind.

"Listen and never judge their worries or concerns. These issues are individual to each person and must be respected as such. And once again, LISTEN."

--Pink Warrior, age 55

Chapter 4

Food is Medicine

I'm in awe of the human body. Lots of thoughts ran through my head during my diagnosis and treatment—some not so cheery—but I never said, "My body is betraying me." I just didn't see it that way. Instead, I thought of it as an incredible machine working hard to get me healthy and back on track. Thanks to our elaborate immune system, which identifies threats such as pathogens and tumor cells, our bodies' first instinct is to fight for us. It wants to heal itself and be well. Think about it in terms of seemingly innocuous, everyday occurrences: an intruder, such as a virus, bacteria, or pollutant, gets into your nose. You sneeze. Into your lungs, you cough. Into your stomach, you vomit. If you cut yourself, platelets hightail it to the wound and plug it up to stop the bleeding. Our bodies are in a constant state of combat for us, never really taking a break. I say give it all the ammunition needed to defend itself, including good nutrition. It's one of the best strategies to prepare for battle.

During chemotherapy, I actually gained weight because of fluid retention (a common side effect) and inactivity during my "dangerous" weeks. An even bigger reason, though, was because I ate every couple of hours as a way to keep the nausea at bay and to get some sustenance. There were many, many times when nothing appealed to me and I had a metal taste in my mouth (another common side effect), which affected how everything tasted. Sometimes I felt so worn out that lifting a fork seemed like a monumental effort. But I forged ahead and forced myself to eat, and with the help of anti-nausea meds, I was able to keep most food down. I'm not saying it's always easy. Heck, no. But at least that's one thing we can control when so much else feels out of whack. I couldn't perform surgery on myself or administer chemo-therapy, but I could determine what to eat, how much, and how often.

Food is medicine 101

One of the biggest allies your friend has in her arsenal for fighting breast cancer is food. We'd all be well-served (again, sorry for the pun) to remember that food is medicine, with preventive and healing properties. It's especially important for your friend to nourish her body when it's under attack from the cancer, or trauma from surgery, radiation, or chemo-therapy.

The link between diet and cancer has been

studied for decades, with evidence suggesting that diet contributes to 20 to 40 percent of all cancers. 29 If the cancer riddle is part genetics and part environmental, this is an impressive figure. Bottom line, we can't choose our biological parents, but many important lifestyle choices, including the food we eat, are within our control. Gaining such an advantage in the fight against cancer is well-worth pursuing.

Although a lengthy discussion of food's chemistry is beyond the scope of this guide, the following are superheroes we should all know a little about in our quest for good health and wellness:

1) **Antioxidants** are substances that protect cells from the damage caused by unstable molecules known as free radicals. 30 Free radicals are chemically reactive because of a missing electron. As a result, they may undergo a process called oxidation, where they take electrons and transfer them, leaving a new free radical. 31 This may cause irreversible damage to DNA and other molecules, leading to diseases such as cancer, unless a free radical scavenger (an antioxidant) stops the process. 32

Common antioxidants include the following:
- beta carotene (found in orange fruits and vegetables, plus some dark, leafy vegetables, such as spinach and kale)

- lycopene (most often associated with tomatoes and tomato products, such as paste, sauce, and juice)

- lutein (found in dark green, leafy vegetables, such as kale, spinach, and greens)

- vitamin A (found in carrots, sweet potatoes, some cheese, and milk)

- vitamin C (found in many fruits and vegetables and some meat)

- vitamin E (found in broccoli and nuts)

2) **Phytochemicals** refer to a wide variety of compounds made by plants with antioxidant properties. [33] Certain phytochemicals may help prevent the formation of potential carcinogens (substances that cause cancer), block the action of carcinogens on their target organs or tissues, or act on cells to suppress cancer development. [34] Evidence for how important phytochemicals are comes from observations of cultures where the diet is plant-based. These countries, including many in Asia, have a lower incidence of cancer than in the United States, where the diet is rich in fatty, processed foods.

Phytochemicals are found in vegetables, fruits, beans, and grains. Although there are thousands of them, only a small fraction has been studied closely, including beta carotene, vitamin C, vitamin E, and folic acid. 35

The lucky 13 super cancer-fighting foods in the next section receive the highest possible marks primarily because of their antioxidant and phytochemical properties.

The lucky 13: super cancer-fighting foods

1) Beans

Never mind the childhood ditty "Beans, beans, the magical fruit, the more you eat, the more you toot." This is one of nature's most perfect foods, full of protein, fiber, selenium, and iron. Beans are also rich in cancer-fighting phytochemicals such as saponins (which keep normal cells from turning into cancer cells and prevent cancer cells from growing); protease inhibitors (protects against disease-causing agents); and phytic acid (enhances immunity and works as an antioxidant to neutralize cell-damaging free radicals). 36 Another bonus is that a wide variety of beans are both accessible and affordable. I can't think of a better food value.

"Bean" recipes in Appendix A include Mum's Minestrone Soup, Mum's Baked Beans, and Hummus.

2) Berries

Blueberries, raspberries, strawberries, and cranberries are among the most delicious sources of vitamin C, an antioxidant that protects against cell damage. As you've read, wacky cells can multiply, replete with errors, and form tumors. Antioxidants are a critical weapon in stopping this process. Berries are also rich in the flavonoid quercetin. A flavonoid is a bioactive plant compound that has antioxidant and anti-inflammatory properties. 37 Blueberries, in particular, pack a powerful nutritional and cancer-preventive punch.

"Berry" recipes in Appendix A include Very Berry Muffins and Lemony Blueberry Zucchini Loaf.

3) Broccoli (and other cruciferous vegetables, such as cauliflower, cabbage, brussels sprouts, turnip, and kale)

Cruciferous vegetables are often mentioned as top cancer fighters, and for good reason: people who eat more of these foods have lower incidences of most cancers. They contain compounds called isothio-cyanates and indoles, which protect healthy cells from everyday stresses and prevent cancer cells from growing. 38 Indoles also act to increase liver enzyme activity that's needed to detoxify carcinogens and other foreign compounds. 39 In addition, the cruciferous family is a good source of vitamins A and C, known for their anti-oxidant properties.

"Broccoli" recipes in Appendix A include Italian Broccoli Casserole and Cheesy Broccoli Cauliflower Soup.

4) Carotenoid-rich fruits and vegetables (such as carrots, squash, pumpkin, cantaloupe, oranges, and sweet potatoes)

Carotenoids, including beta-carotene, are rich in vitamins A and C, which are powerful antioxidants. They help regulate cell differentiation (cancer cells are characterized by lack of differentiation), inhibit the proliferation of cancer cells and tumor growth, and enhance immune function. 40 This large group of fruits and vegetables is highly versatile and easily accessible, available fresh throughout the year.

"Carotenoid-rich" recipes in Appendix A include Carrot Ginger Soup, Curry Butternut Squash Soup, and Sweet Potato Pie.

5) Dark green, leafy vegetables (such as spinach, Swiss chard, mustard greens, lettuce, and kale)

This group of vegetables is an excellent source of fiber, folate, and a wide range of carotenoids that take care of potentially dangerous free radicals in the body before they can do harm. 41 In addition, some laboratory research found that the carotenoids in dark green, leafy vegetables can inhibit the growth of certain types of breast cancer cells. 42 An added bonus is that this group of vegetables contains kaempferol, a flavonoid phyto-nutrient; women who eat the most kaempferol-rich foods have a 40% lower risk of developing ovarian cancer than those with the lowest intake of kaempferol-rich foods. 43

"Dark green, leafy vegetable" recipes in Appendix A include My Spanakopitta (Spinach Pie) and Kale Tomato Pie.

6) Fish

Omega-3 fatty acids—found in fatty fish such as salmon, tuna, trout, mackerel, anchovies, sardines, swordfish, and striped bass—are known for their cardiovascular health benefits, but may decrease breast cancer cell growth, too. Researchers have proposed that omega-3 fatty acids affect prostaglandins, which in turn modulate the immune response, blood supply, and cell membrane integrity in decreasing breast cancer cell growth. [44] Specifically, fish seems to protect against cancer by restricting the production of prostaglandins, inflammatory compounds that act as tumor promoters. [45] However, some species, particularly the large, predator fish such as swordfish and tuna, should not be consumed more than once a week due to elevated mercury levels.

"Fish" recipes in Appendix A include Mum's Maine Fish Chowder and Mum's Baked, Creamed Fish.

7) Grapes

Both grapes and grape juice (red and purple, in particular) are rich sources of resveratrol, a type of natural phytochemical that belongs to a much larger group of phytochemicals called polyphenols. [46] With potent antioxidant and anti-inflammatory properties, resveratrol has been shown to slow the growth of cancer cells and inhibit the formation of tumors in breast cells. [47]

A recipe for Curry Chicken Salad can be found in Appendix A. Also, don't forget to include grapes in fruit salads, and for a sweet treat that helps with sore throats, freeze them!

8) Green tea

Green tea contains powerful antioxidants, including polyphenols and flavonoids, which have been shown to slow cancer development in breast cells. [48] Specifically, polyphenols help eliminate free radicals that can alter DNA, causing cell mutation and leading to cancer formation. [49] A January, 2009 study on tea consumption and breast cancer in Cancer Epidemiology, Biomarkers, and Prevention revealed that drinking three cups or more of tea per day was associated with a thirty-seven percent decrease in breast cancer risk in women under the age of fifty. [50] A note of caution, however: high dosages of green tea supplements may interact with certain medications.

A Tropical Quinoa Pudding recipe (made with green tea) can be found in Appendix A.

9) Mushrooms

Mushrooms are packed with important minerals and vitamins, including the antioxidant selenium, which can protect against cancer, and vitamin D (in fact, mushrooms are the only fruit or vegetable that contain vitamin D). Certain varieties also contain polysaccharides, substances that may stimulate the immune system and provide anti-cancer protection by recognizing and destroying cancer cells, viruses, and bacteria. [51] Shiitake and maitake mushrooms contain the polysaccharides lentinan and beta-glucan, respectively. Each activates the body's immune system; beta-glucan appears to increase the action of natural killer (NK) cells, which regulate immune system responses and cause the death of tumor cells. [52] On a practical note, mushrooms are wonderfully versatile and easy to incorporate in a variety of dishes.

"Mushroom" recipes in Appendix A include

Mushroom Lasagna and Cream of Mushroom Soup.

10) Onions (and other vegetables in the allium family, such as garlic, shallots, scallions, chives, and leeks)

Allium vegetables contain many cancer-suppressing agents such as quercetn, allixin, and a large group of organosulfur compounds that includes allicin, alliin, and allyl sulfides. [53] Allyl sulfides work to increase toxin-eliminating enzymes in the liver that sweep cancer-causing chemical substances (procarcinogens) out of the body. [54] These compounds also increase the activity of certain immune system cells, such as macrophages and T lymphocytes. [55] One garlic component, diallyl disulfide, has demonstrated potent preventive effects against cancer in the laboratory. [56] As with mushrooms, this group of vegetables is easy to incorporate in a variety of dishes.

"Onion" recipes in Appendix A include Rebecca's Stuffing Bread and Potato Leek Soup.

11) Nuts and Seeds (notably walnuts and flaxseed)

Nuts are nutritional treasures, full of protein and vitamins, as well as antioxidants such as quercetin and capferol that may suppress cancer's growth. [57] Vitamin E, which protects the body from cell damage and works with other antioxidants such as vitamin C to ward off chronic diseases, is found in nuts and seeds. [58] Nuts are also a good source of selenium, which enhances the antioxidant activity of vitamin E, increases immune response, and may alter metabolism of carcinogens so they produce less toxic substances. 59 Flaxseed is a rich source of lignans, compounds that are transformed by the bacteria in our bodies into hormone-like substances (phytoestrogens) that may protect against tumor formation and growth. 60 Further, the lignan content of flaxseed is up to 800 times greater than that of other plant food. 61 Another bonus is that nuts, in particular, are the ultimate convenience food—easy to pack and eat on the go, or sneak into pasta, salads, or breads.

"Nut" recipes in Appendix A include Nut-Stuffed Chicken with Pineapple and Almond Spinach Manicotti.

12) Quinoa and whole grains

The term "whole grain" means that all three parts of the grain kernel (germ, bran, and endosperm) are included, whereas refined grains usually have the germ and bran removed, leaving only the starchy endosperm. 62 In addition to being rich in fiber, vitamins, and minerals, whole grains contain substances known to reduce cancer risk, including antioxidants and phytochemicals (specifically, phenols, lignans, and saponins). 63 Women who eat lignan-rich foods, for example, are less likely to develop breast cancer than those with lower consumption levels. 64 Scientists believe that fiber may hamper the growth of some early-stage breast tumors by binding with estrogen in the intestine, decreasing the amount of excess estrogen from being reabsorbed from the intestines and pumped into the bloodstream. 65

Quinoa (KEEN-wah) looks like a grain and is prepared as such, but is actually more closely related to spinach and Swiss chard. This nutritional powerhouse contains all nine essential amino acids, making it a complete protein. Lysine, an amino acid essential for tissue growth and cellular repair, is abundant in quinoa. Native to South America, it was once called the "gold of the Incas."

"Quinoa" recipes in Appendix A include Whole Grain Mac 'n Cheese and Creamy Pesto Asparagus Quinoa.

13) Tomatoes

Tomatoes routinely make cancer-fighting food lists, in large part because of their abundance of the powerful phytochemical lycopene. Lycopene acts as a potent antioxidant to stop free radicals from tearing through the body's cell membranes and harming the DNA. [66] Lycopene also helps restore the normal cellular communication that is lacking in tumors; specifically, when cells are able to communicate, cancer cells can be signaled to halt their growth. [67] Although much attention has been given to lycopene's cancer fighting properties for prostate cancer, tomato components have also stopped the proliferation of several other cancer cell types, including breast, in laboratory studies. [68]

The good news for those who don't care for raw tomatoes is that when in a processed form (sauce, paste, or juice), lycopene and other components are released and more easily absorbed. This makes the tomato one of the most versatile super foods, easily found in well-liked dishes such as spaghetti, lasagna, and pizza.

"Tomato" recipes in Appendix A include

Tomato-Basil Soup, Green Gazpacho, and Christian Granger's Red Sauce.

Honorable Mention:
Avocados

As with the other super foods discussed before, avocados are chock full of vitamins, minerals, anti-oxidants, and phytochemicals. Notable vitamins found in avocados include E, K, and B6, which are beneficial for healthy cell function and cancer prevention. Carotenoids, including lutein, are also found in avocados and are known to inhibit the growth of breast cancer cells. Avocados also contain the master antioxidant, glutathione, which helps the liver effectively detoxify the body and protect cells from oxidative stress. [69] In addition, the healthy, monounsaturated fats that avocados are known for facilitate the absorption of phytochemicals both within the avocado and from other vegetables and fruits. [70]

"Avocado" recipes in Appendix A include Yummy Guacamole and Kicky Cucumber Avocado Soup.

Final Thoughts

"Breast cancer is a horrible, life-altering, life-stealing disease that is poorly understood. Between surgery, treatment, and long-term medications...and side effects... and the haunting of possible recurrence...it is just a terrible, awful thing. I think that all breast cancer survivors will say they are doing well...as well as they can...but it has created a heaviness in your heart and soul that will never go away. It also has forced me to look at each day as a gift, an opportunity to love for one more day, to plant one more rose bush, to make one more phone call to distant friends..."
--Kimberly B., age 55

I like this quote, because it beautifully summarizes many women's breast cancer experiences. Cancer is frightening and completely disruptive, but what can be gained from the illness is truly remarkable.

I'm writing this exactly one year after my last chemotherapy treatment. One of my nightly rituals is to reflect on the many blessings in my life, which includes those who walked with me during the trials and triumphs of the past year and a half. Trust me, you have an extraordinary opportunity to make your friend's journey lighter and more loving with the warmth and care you provide. Take the time to reach out often and encourage her warrior spirit. She'll be grateful for the rest of her life.

I wish you and your friend the very best.

A Word on Those Who Don't Make it

It's gut-wrenching to include this page, because my wish is that every woman who is diagnosed not only survives breast cancer, but thrives after treatment. Unfortunately, that doesn't always happen. According to the American Cancer Society, about forty thousand women in the United States die from the disease each year. 71 These sister warriors bravely fight cancer's battles but ultimately don't win the war. We must honor them by the way in which we live our lives, full of gratitude and grace, and never forgetting their indomitable spirit.

Grief is an extremely personal experience, and we each search for comfort in our own, unique way. As you are aware, end of life issues are not the focus of this book. However, I know those who have found solace in the work of Elisabeth Kubler-Ross when seeking answers about the grieving process.

If someone you love has been taken by this disease, please know that the community of breast cancer sisters holds you in our hearts and is deeply sorry for your loss.

Appendix A

Recipes For All Stages of Her Battle

The following recipes are comfort foods. Unfussy, simple, and easy to make, they're ones my family, friends, and I have enjoyed before, during, and after my cancer treatment. All contain some combination of the 13 super cancer-fighting foods discussed previously. These foods are great during any phase of your friend's illness, and some are particularly helpful when she's experiencing a spectrum of side effects from radiation or chemotherapy (including nausea, mouth sores, diarrhea, constipation, sore throat, fatigue, and lack of appetite).

With the exception of the Very Berry Muffins and the Lemony Blueberry Zucchini Loaf, each recipe can be tweaked according to your friend's preferences and the ingredients available to you. Although most of the dishes are vegetarian, you can easily slip chicken or another meat into many of them. Also, most (with the exception of those using phyllo dough) can be frozen. Your friend will appreciate your culinary efforts now and later on when she's just not up to cooking.

Mum's Minestrone Soup

You'll need:
- 1 cup of mixed dried beans
- 3 tablespoons of beef or vegetable bouillon
- 1 large onion, sliced or diced any way you choose
- 3 ribs of celery, sliced
- 1 to 1 and ½ cups of carrots, sliced
- 1 to 1 and ½ cups of canned or frozen green beans
- 1 quart of stewed tomatoes
- 1/3 cup of olive oil
- Generous amount of garlic, fresh or powdered
- Approximately 2 cups of pasta (spaghetti, cheese-filled tortellini, whatever you'd like)
- Any leftover vegetables in your refrigerator that you'd like to use: mashed potato, turnip, squash, etc.
- A handful of fresh spinach
- Small amounts of Italian spice, salt, and pepper

1) Soak the beans in a large pot for a few hours or overnight. You can also cover with water and start cooking without soaking, but it takes much longer.
2) Add the bouillon.
3) After the beans have been simmered gently to nearly a soft stage, add all of your vegetables, olive oil, and garlic.
4) After vegetables are soft, add a small amount of Italian spice, salt, and pepper, but not too much until

you have sampled the broth.

5) Add pasta and simmer until cooked. You can get creative and add leftover meatballs, Italian sausage, etc. if you'd like.

Mum's Baked Beans

You'll need:

- 2 pounds (4 cups) of dry beans (navy, pea, yellow-eye, soldier, Jacob's cattle, red kidney, etc.)
- 1/3 to ½ cup of olive oil
- 1/3 to ½ cup of molasses
- 1/3 to ½ cup of apple cider vinegar
- 2 teaspoons of salt
- 1 heaping tablespoon of dry mustard
- Pepper to taste
- Meat, such as boneless chicken breasts or a small, boneless pork roast (optional)

1) Rinse beans in a large pot with warm water and drain. Cover beans in cold water and let set overnight or for about 6 hours.

2) When they've swollen to absorb most of the water, add all of the other ingredients (except meat) and stir.

Bake at 325° for 6 hours in a metal pot (with lid). If adding meat, place on top of the beans halfway through the baking process and cover.

Note: keep beans covered with water the first hour or two, then let them bake a little dry so they'll brown up. You can add more water the last several hours to create juice that's thick. To speed up step 1, you can also heat the beans, water, and other ingredients on top of the stove until they swell (simmering gently for about an hour), then bake them at 325° for 6 hours.

Hummus

You'll need:
- (2) 15.5 ounce cans of chick peas, drained (but save the liquid)
- 2 tablespoons of tahini paste (100% ground sesame)
- 3 garlic cloves, minced
- 2 lemons
- 2 teaspoons of ground cumin
- 2 tablespoons of olive oil
- Salt and pepper to taste, paprika for color

1) Place all ingredients except the paprika in a bowl and mix using an immersion blender until smooth, gradually adding the chick pea liquid until it's the consistency you prefer.
2) Add more salt and pepper if needed and sprinkle paprika for color. Refrigerate.

This is the basic hummus recipe I use, but I like to vary it, too, by adding the following ingredients before I blend.
"Greek" style hummus: kalamata olives, green pepper, and feta cheese
"Red" hummus: either roasted red pepper or sun dried tomatoes
"Kicky green" hummus: cilantro and jalapeno pepper

Serve with soft pita bread, pita chips, or a variety of raw vegetables.

Very Berry Muffins

You'll need:
- 1 cup of fresh blueberries
- 1 cup of fresh raspberries
- ½ cup of fresh strawberries, chopped fine
- 2 and 1/4 cups of flour
- 1 and ½ cups of sugar
- ½ cup of butter, melted
- 2 eggs, beaten
- 3/4 cup of milk
- 2 teaspoons of vanilla
- 1 to 2 teaspoons of cinnamon
- 2 teaspoons of baking powder
- 1 teaspoon of salt
- Cooking spray for muffin tins

1) Heat oven to 450°, then reduce to 400° when putting the muffins in to bake.
2) Combine the flour, sugar, cinnamon, baking powder, and salt in one bowl, mix well.
3) In another bowl, combine the butter, eggs, milk, and vanilla, beat well.
4) Add the dry ingredients to the wet until just blended, careful not to over mix.
5) Gently fold the berries into the batter.
6) Generously coat muffin tins with cooking spray and fill ¾ full.

Bake for approximately 20 minutes.

Yields 18 muffins
*Note: tips to avoid flat-top muffins include 1) not over-filling the tins, 2) not over-mixing the batter, and 3) not using muffin papers. Also, skilled muffin makers suggest having an oven that is too hot, then reducing to the correct temperature when placing the muffins in to bake.

Lemony Blueberry Zucchini Loaf

You'll need:
- 1 cup of blueberries
- 2 cups of peeled, shredded zucchini
- 3 eggs
- ¾ cup of vegetable oil
- 1 and ½ cups of sugar
- 2 teaspoons of lemon extract
- 2 and ½ cups of flour
- 1 teaspoon of salt
- ½ teaspoon of nutmeg
- ¼ teaspoon of ginger
- 1 teaspoon of baking soda
- 2 teaspoons of baking powder
- 1 cup of chopped walnuts (optional)
- Crisco

1) Heat oven to 350°. Grease only the bottom of two glass loaf pans with Crisco.
2) In one bowl, beat the eggs, then add vegetable oil, sugar, and lemon extract until well blended.
3) In another bowl, sift the flour, salt, nutmeg, ginger, baking soda, and baking powder.
4) Add the dry ingredients to the wet and mix until

well-incorporated, then fold in the zucchini, then blueberries and walnuts. Pour into the two loaf pans.

Bake for about 50 minutes or until a toothpick comes out clean.

Italian Broccoli Casserole

You'll need:
- (2) 10-ounce packages of frozen broccoli
- 2 eggs, beaten well
- (1) 11-ounce can of cheddar cheese soup
- 1 teaspoon of oregano
- (1) 8-ounce can of stewed tomatoes, Italian style
- 3 tablespoons of grated parmesan cheese
- 1 tablespoon of butter
- Ground black pepper to taste

1) Butter a casserole/baking dish.
2) In large bowl, mix the beaten eggs, cheddar cheese soup, and oregano until completely blended.
3) Gently fold in the broccoli and stewed tomatoes.
4) Pour in casserole dish and sprinkle the grated parmesan over the top, with black pepper to taste.

Bake uncovered at 350° for 30 minutes.

Cheesy Broccoli and Cauliflower Soup

You'll need:
- 4 cups of broccoli florets
- 4 cups of cauliflower florets
- 1 cup of chopped onions
- 2 large carrots, diced well

- 4 cups of medium cheddar cheese, grated or cubed
- 3 cups of skim milk
- 6 tablespoons of butter
- ½ cup of flour
- 3 cups of water
- 3 Knorr's vegetarian stock cubes (or chicken stock)

1) In a large pot, cook the carrots and chopped onions in the vegetable stock until tender.
2) Add the broccoli and cauliflower and simmer until tender, careful not to overcook.
3) In a separate pan, melt butter. Remove from heat and add the flour, blending well.
4) Add the milk to the butter/flour mixture and continue cooking over medium heat.
5) Once the milk starts to gently bubble, add cheese and stir constantly to avoid burning.
6) When the cheese is melted, pour into the pot of vegetables and stir well.

Yields about 10 cups

Carrot Ginger Soup

You'll need:
- 6 cups of water
- 3 Knorr's vegetarian stock cubes
- 4 cups of chopped carrots
- 1 cup of chopped shallots
- 4 tablespoons of ginger
- 2 cloves of garlic

- 1 can of coconut milk (13.5 ounces)
- 2 tablespoons of olive oil

1) Cook the carrots in the vegetable broth until very soft.
2) Sautee shallots, ginger, and garlic in the olive oil until soft.
3) Remove the carrots from heat and add shallots, ginger, garlic, and coconut milk. Once cooled a bit, use an immersion blender or regular blender to puree.

Yields 6 cups

Curry Butternut Squash Soup

You'll need:
- 6 cups of water
- 3 Knorr's vegetarian stock cubes
- 6 to 7 cups of peeled, cubed butternut squash
- 2 cups of peeled, chopped apples
- 1 cup of chopped onions
- 4 cloves of minced garlic
- 2 tablespoons of olive oil
- 2 tablespoons of ground curry
- 1 can of evaporated milk (12 ounces)

1) Boil squash and apples in vegetable stock until very soft.
2) Sautee onions and garlic in olive oil until soft.
3) Remove the squash and apples from heat and add onions, garlic, curry, and evaporated milk. Once cooled a bit, use an immersion blender or regular blender to puree.

Yields 10 cups

Sweet Potato Pie (with phyllo dough)

You'll need:

- 4 to 5 cups of mashed sweet potato (about 6 cups of peeled and cubed sweet potato before cooking/mashing)
- 1 package of phyllo dough, thawed
- (2) 4-ounce packages of crumbled bleu cheese
- ½ to ¾ cup of dried cranberries
- ½ cup of brown sugar
- 1 cup of chopped walnuts
- 2 teaspoons of cinnamon
- ½ cup of melted butter
- 2 tablespoons of olive oil

1) Grease a 13 X 9 glass casserole dish with olive oil and place half of the phyllo dough down.
2) Mix the brown sugar, cinnamon, and mashed sweet potato until well-blended.
3) Spread this mixture evenly over the phyllo dough.
4) Sprinkle the bleu cheese, walnuts, and cranberries evenly over the sweet potato mixture and cover with the remaining phyllo dough.
5) Spread the melted butter over the top of the phyllo dough, making sure that it's completely moistened.

Bake at 375°for approximately 45 minutes or until the phyllo dough becomes crispy and turns a deep, golden brown color.

Spanakopitta (Spinach Pie)

You'll need:

- 1 package of phyllo dough (2 typically come in a box, only use one), thawed (takes about ½ hour)
- 2 boxes of chopped, frozen spinach
- 12 eggs, beaten well
- 2 blocks of feta cheese
- ½ cup of butter, melted
- 1 packet of hollandaise sauce mix
- 3-4 tablespoons of olive oil
- 3-4 lemons
- Garlic powder and black pepper to taste

1) Grease a 13 X 9 casserole dish with the olive oil.
2) Lay half of the phyllo sheets on the bottom of the dish.
3) Pour the beaten eggs over the sheets.
4) Thaw the spinach in microwave for a few minutes. While still in the box, squeeze all of the water out. (I usually wring the box like a dishrag). You'll want the spinach as dry as possible.
5) Lay the spinach evenly over the eggs.
6) Slice the feta cheese and lay evenly over the spinach.
7) Lay the other half of phyllo dough on top of the feta cheese.
8) In a small bowl, melt the butter. Add the hollandaise sauce powder, juice from a few lemons, black pepper, and some garlic powder (approximately a tablespoon), and mix well.
9) Pour over the phyllo dough and spread evenly. Be sure that all of the phyllo dough is moistened.

Bake at 375° for approximately 30 minutes. Keep checking the phyllo dough, which should turn crispy and golden to dark brown. Let set for 10 to 15 minutes and serve with lemon wedges. When re-heating, use an oven instead of a microwave so that the phyllo dough comes back to life (crispy).

Kale Tomato Pie

You'll need:
- (1) 9-inch frozen pie shell (deep)
- 2 cups of fresh, packed kale (only the flowered part, not the spine)
- 3 Roma tomatoes
- 4 cloves of garlic
- 1/3 cup of walnuts
- ½ cup of shredded parmesan cheese
- ½ cup of olive oil
- 2/3 cup of ricotta cheese
- 4 ounces of shredded mozzarella cheese
- Salt and pepper to taste
- A food processor or sturdy blender

1) Heat oven to 375° and bake pie shell for 10 minutes (this prevents the bottom from becoming soggy later on).
2) In a food processor or blender, create a pesto using the olive oil, kale, garlic, walnuts, parmesan cheese.
3) In a bowl, mix the kale pesto and ricotta cheese until well blended.
4) Pour pesto in the pie shell and then layer with sliced tomatoes.
5) Add salt and pepper to taste.

6) Top with shredded mozzarella cheese.
Bake for about 40 minutes or until the cheese is golden brown.
*Note: I've also used the kale pesto for stuffing peppers. Cut the sides of yellow, red, orange, and green peppers into mini-bowl-like pieces (usually I can get three from one pepper). Coat baking sheet with olive oil and bake the stuffed peppers (with mozzarella on top) at 400° until the cheese is golden brown.

My Mother's Maine Fish Chowder

You'll need:

- 4 cups of any white potatoes (approximately 4 medium potatoes), peeled and cubed
- 1 cup of yellow or white onions (approximately 1 medium onion), coarsely chopped
- 1 pound of mild-flavored white fish (haddock, pollack, cod), fresh or frozen
- 1 can of evaporated milk (12 ounces)
- 1 tablespoon of butter
- ½ teaspoon of ground thyme
- 1 teaspoon of salt
- Ground black pepper

1) Cook potatoes and onions in salted water (water should just cover the vegetables) until nearly soft.
2) Lay the fish on top of the potato/onion mixture and continue cooking at low heat (simmer) until the fish is opaque, approximately 15 minutes.
3) Add butter, thyme, and pepper to taste.

Mum's Baked, Creamed Fish

You'll need:

- 1 pound of any mild white fish, fresh or frozen
- 1 and ½ cups of skim milk
- ½ cup of sharp cheddar cheese, grated
- Approximately 4 tablespoons of melted butter
- 1 and ½ tablespoons of corn starch
- ½ cup of crushed cheddar or Ritz crackers
- 1 tablespoon of cooking sherry

1) Butter a shallow casserole dish and place pieces of the fish in a single layer (not stacked on top of each other).

2) In a saucepan, make the cheesy white sauce by dissolving the corn starch in a tablespoon of butter, then adding the milk and whisking over medium heat. Make sure there are no corn starch lumps. Once thickened, add the cheese and whip so not to burn on the bottom. Add sherry (optional) and mix well.

3) Pour sauce over the fish so that each piece is completely covered.

4) In a small bowl, mix 2 tablespoons of melted butter and cracker crumbs well, and sprinkle over the top of the sauce.

Bake at 375° for 30 minutes.

Curry Chicken Salad

You'll need:

- 2 chicken breasts
- 8 tablespoons of mayonnaise
- 4 teaspoons of ground curry

- 2 dozen purple grapes, halved
- ½ cup of crushed walnuts
- 2 teaspoons of chicken bouillon
- 2 tablespoons of olive oil
- Pepper to taste

1) Place chicken breasts on top of olive oil in a baking/casserole dish.
2) Sprinkle the chicken bouillon over the breasts and add a few tablespoons of water.
3) Cover tightly with aluminum foil and bake at 325° for one hour. When cooled completely, refrigerate chicken in its juice until chilled.
4) Mix the mayonnaise and curry until blended, then add the grapes and walnuts.
3) Cut the chicken in whatever size pieces you'd like and fold into the curry mixture. Add pepper to taste and serve alone, on a bed of greens, or in sandwiches.

Tropical Quinoa Pudding Made with Green Tea

You'll need:
- 1 cup of dry quinoa
- 2 cups of green tea
- 2 cups of chopped mango or pineapple (or 1 cup of each)
- 1 cup of chopped walnuts
- 1 cup of shredded coconut
- 2 cups of coconut milk
- 4 eggs, beaten
- ½ teaspoon of cinnamon
- 1 and ½ to 2 cups of brown sugar

- 2 teaspoons of coconut or almond extract

1) Bring the green tea and quinoa to a boil, then cover and simmer until the green tea is absorbed.
2) In large bowl, mix eggs, mango, pineapple, walnuts, ½ cup of shredded coconut, coconut milk, cinnamon, brown sugar, and coconut (or almond) extract.
3) Pour into lightly-greased casserole dish and sprinkle ½ cup of shredded coconut on top.

Bake at 375° for 30 minutes.
*Note: To bring back to life the following day(s), add milk and heat in the microwave.

Mushroom Lasagna

You'll need:
- 8 cups of sliced mushrooms (any combination of button, portobello, cremini, shiitake, etc.)
- 10 sheets of cooked lasagna
- 3 and ½ cups of whole milk
- 4 cups of smoked gouda cheese, grated or cut into small pieces
- 1 cup of grated parmesan cheese
- 1 cup of walnuts, chopped very fine
- 2 shallots, chopped
- 3 garlic cloves, minced
- 6 tablespoons of olive oil
- 4 tablespoons of butter
- 1 Knorrs vegetable stock cube
- 1 and ½ cups of water
- 3 tablespoons of flour

1) In large pan, sauté the mushrooms, shallots, garlic, and mushrooms in the olive oil over medium heat until tender.
2) Add the vegetable stock cube and water, and continue cooking until the liquid is almost gone. Set aside.
3) In medium-sized pot, melt the butter over high heat. Once bubbling, stir in the flour completely. Add the milk and stir constantly until thickened.
4) Add the smoked gouda and stir continuously until completely melted. Set aside.
5) Lightly grease a 13 X 9 casserole dish and place three of the lasagna sheets.
6) Pour a third of the cheese sauce over the lasagna sheets, then ½ of the mushroom/shallot/garlic mixture. Cover with 3 more lasagna sheets.
7) Pour another third of the cheese sauce over the lasagna sheets, then the remaining mushroom/shallot/garlic mixture. Cover with 3 or 4 lasagna sheets and the remaining third of cheese sauce.
8) Mix the parmesan cheese and crushed walnuts in a bowl, then spread evenly over the top of the lasagna.

Bake at 350° for 45 minutes. Let stand for 10 to 15 minutes before serving.

Cream of Mushroom Soup
You'll need:
- 6 cups of sliced mushrooms (variety—button, portobello, etc.)
- 3 cloves of garlic, minced
- 2 shallots, chopped well

- 6 tablespoons of butter
- 2 tablespoons of flour
- 2 cups of whole milk
- 2 Knorr's vegetable stock cubes
- 1 and ½ cups of water
- 1 tablespoon of sherry

1) Sautee the mushrooms, garlic, and shallots in 4 tablespoons of butter until tender.
2) In a medium-sized pot, melt 2 tablespoons of butter and add flour, blending well.
3) Add milk and cook over medium-high heat until thickened.
4) Make vegetable stock with cubes and 1 and ½ cups of water.
5) Add vegetable stock, mushrooms, shallots, garlic, and sherry to the milk mixture and stir thoroughly.
6) Either leave the soup as is or use an immersion blender to eliminate pieces of mushroom and shallots.

Yields 5 cups

Rebecca's Stuffing Bread

My cousin Rebecca introduced this bread to our family, and it's always a big hit with everyone who tries it. You'll need:

- 1/3 cup of finely chopped onion
- 1/3 cup of finely chopped celery
- 2 tablespoons of yeast
- 2 tablespoons of honey
- ½ teaspoon of celery seed
- ¾ teaspoon of sage

- ¾ teaspoon of pepper
- 1 heaping teaspoon of poultry seasoning
- 1 heaping teaspoon of thyme
- 1 heaping teaspoon of salt
- 2 tablespoons of olive oil
- 1 and ½ cup of hot water
- 1 cup of hot chicken stock (or vegetable stock)
- 7 cups of all-purpose flour
- Crisco

1) Mix the honey, celery, onion, celery seed, sage, pepper, poultry seasoning, thyme, salt, olive oil, water, and chicken stock.

2) When cooled to just warm, add the yeast.

3) Add half of the flour. Blend until smooth with a hand mixer, then add as much flour as you can mix in. Complete the addition of flour by kneading it on the counter, ½ a cup at a time, until you have formed a smooth ball.

4) Coat a large bowl with olive oil and roll the ball of dough around so it's completely coated.

5) Cover bowl top with plastic wrap and let the ball of dough double in size.

6) Grease 3 loaf pans with Crisco. *Note: don't use butter (it burns) or cooking spray (it's not substantial enough)

7) Once the ball of dough has doubled in size, punch it down and form 3 balls of dough. Place them in the greased loaf pans and let double in size again.

Bake at 350° for 30 to 45 minutes if using glass loaf pans, and 375° if using metal ones. You'll know that it's done if you tap on the top of the loaves and hear a hollow sound. Remove immediately from the loaf pans and cool on a baking rack.

Yields 3 large loaves

Potato Leek Soup

You'll need:
- 4 cups of peeled, chopped white potatoes
- 2 cups of chopped leeks
- 4 tablespoons of butter
- ½ cup of chopped chives
- 4 cloves of garlic, minced
- 4 sprigs of thyme
- 1 cup of white wine
- ¾ cup of heavy cream
- 4 Knorr's vegetarian stock cubes
- 1 cup of crisp, crumbled bacon (optional)

1) In large pot, boil potatoes, Knorr's cubes, and leeks until tender in 4 cups of water. Set aside.
2) Sautee butter, chives, garlic, and sprigs of thyme until tender. Once cooled, strip thyme from stick.
3) Combine all ingredients in the pot and then add the wine, heavy cream, and bacon (if not doing the vegetarian version).
4) Liquefy all ingredients with a blender (immersion or regular).
5) Add pepper to taste and garnish with fresh chives.

Yields about 8 cups

Cucumber Yogurt Dill Soup
(cold, great for a sore throat)

You'll need:
- 2 cups of peeled and shredded cucumber
- 2 cups of low fat, plain yogurt
- ¼ packed cup of finely chopped fresh dill, no stems
- ¼ cup of finely chopped fresh mint, no stems
- 2 tablespoons of red wine vinegar
- 1 teaspoon of salt
- 2 tablespoons of olive oil
- 3 garlic cloves, minced

1) Sautee garlic in the olive oil until tender.
2) Remove from heat and cool.
3) Mix all of the ingredients and keep chilled.

Yields 7 cups

Nut-Stuffed Chicken with Pineapple

You'll need:
- 5 or 6 thin chicken cutlets (pounded down will do the trick)
- 1/3 cup of crushed walnuts, pecans, or macadamia nuts
- ¼ cup of peeled, finely-chopped apple, any variety
- ¼ cup of shredded coconut
- (1) 8-ounce can of crushed pineapple
- ½ cup of white wine
- 2 tablespoons of butter
- 3 tablespoons of flour

- 2 chicken bouillons
- 1 cup of water

1) Mix the nuts, apple, coconut, and ½ of the pineapple in a bowl (reserve the pineapple juice for sauce).
2) Place a few tablespoons of the nut/fruit mixture on each cutlet and roll (like a jellyroll, starting at the narrow end). Set aside.
3) In a saucepan, melt the butter and add the flour, blending well.
4) Add wine, water, chicken bouillons, and the remaining pineapple/pineapple juice. Cook over medium heat until thickened into a sauce.
5) Pour enough sauce on the bottom of a casserole dish to coat. Place chicken rolls in the dish and cover with the sauce.

Cover with tinfoil and bake at 350° for approximately 45 minutes.

Almond Spinach Manicotti

You'll need:
- 10 manicotti shells
- ½ cup of sliced almonds
- 2 cups of fresh spinach, cut in strips (no stems)
- 2 eggs, beaten
- 15 ounces of ricotta cheese
- ½ cup of fresh basil, cut in strips (no stems)
- 1 cup of fresh, chopped mushrooms
- ¼ cup of chopped shallots or other onion
- 2 cloves of garlic
- 2 tablespoons of olive oil

- 1 teaspoon of salt
- (1) 15-ounce jar of Alfredo sauce
- ½ cup of shredded parmesan cheese

1) Bring a pot of water to a boil and cook the manicotti shells until tender. Rinse in cold water and set aside.
2) Sautee the garlic, mushrooms, shallots, and spinach in olive oil until tender.
2) In a bowl, mix the eggs, salt, ricotta cheese, fresh basil, and ¼ cup of the sliced almonds. Fold in the mushroom mixture until well blended.
3) Lightly coat the bottom of a 13 X 9 glass baking dish with some of the Alfredo sauce (not too much).
4) Stuff the manicotti shells with the filling and place in baking dish.
5) Pour the remaining Alfredo sauce over the shells.
6) Sprinkle ¼ cup of the sliced almonds and the parmesan cheese on top.

Cover with tin foil and bake at 350°for about 30 minutes. Let set for 15 minutes before serving.

Whole Grain Mac 'n Cheese

You'll need:
- 13.25 ounce box of whole grain penne pasta or whole grain elbow macaroni (equivalent to 4 dry cups)
- ½ cup of unsalted butter
- 4 tablespoons of flour
- 2 cups of whole milk
- 3 cups of cheese (I like to use 1 and ½ cups of a creamy cheese, such as harvarti, and 1 and ½ cups

of a flavorful cheese, such as smoked gouda)
- ½ cup of bread crumbs
- ½ teaspoon of ground ginger

1) Lightly grease a 13 X 9 glass casserole dish.
2) Bring a pot of water to boil and cook pasta until tender, drain and set aside.
3) Melt ¼ cup of butter in a medium-sized pot. Add flour and mix well, until you have a paste.
4) Add milk and stir constantly over medium heat until it thickens.
5) Add all of the cheese and stir constantly until it's melted.
6) Mix the melted cheese, pasta, and ginger. Pour into the casserole dish.
7) In a bowl, melt ¼ cup of butter and mix with the bread crumbs.
8) Sprinkle evenly over the top of the macaroni and cheese.

Bake at 350° for about 30 minutes. Let set for 15 minutes before serving.

Creamy Pesto Asparagus Quinoa
You'll need:
- 1 and ½ cups of uncooked quinoa
- 3 cups of vegetable or chicken broth
- 2 cups of asparagus tips (about 2 bunches worth of tips)
- 6 tablespoons of pesto
- 2 tablespoons of olive oil
- 1 package (8 ounces) of cream cheese

- ½ cup of sliced almonds
- Pepper to taste

1) Bring broth and quinoa to a boil, then cover and simmer until all of the broth is absorbed.
2) Sautee asparagus tips in olive oil until tender.
3) Melt cream cheese in microwave until soft, then thoroughly mix with the pesto.
4) Combine the quinoa, cream cheese/pesto mixture, and asparagus tips and fold into a lightly-greased casserole dish.
5) Sprinkle sliced almonds over the top.

Bake at 350° for about 30 minutes.
*Note that this will remind you of a super-creamy risotto.

Tomato Basil Soup

You'll need:
- 6 cups of roma tomatoes (18 to 20)
- 2 cups of water
- 3 Knorr's vegetable stock cubes
- 6 ounces of tomato paste
- 1 cup of fresh, chopped basil
- ½ cup of white wine
- 1 can of evaporated milk (12 ounces)
- 1 to 1 and ½ cups of chopped onion
- 2 garlic cloves
- 2 tablespoons of olive oil

1) Bring vegetable stock and tomatoes to a boil and then cook over medium heat until very soft.

2) Add tomato paste and basil and continue cooking until tender.

3) Sautee onion and garlic in olive oil until soft and add to tomatoes and basil.

4) Remove from heat and once cooled, use an immersion blender or regular blender to puree.

5) Use a sieve to remove seeds.

6) Add white wine and evaporated milk to tomato mixture and mix well.

Yields 10 cups

Green Gazpacho
(cold, great for a sore throat)

You'll need:

- 4 cups of skinned Roma tomatoes
- 3 garlic cloves, minced
- 1 green pepper, chopped, no seeds
- 1 jalapeno pepper, chopped
- ¼ cup of fresh parsley, chopped, no stems
- ¼ cup of fresh basil, chopped, no stems
- 1 and ½ cups of peeled cucumber, diced
- 4 tablespoons of red wine vinegar
- 4 tablespoons of olive oil

1) Liquefy all of the ingredients in a blender.

2) Chill and serve cold. You can also garnish with tiny pieces of onion, green pepper, tomato, cucumber, and garlic croutons.

Yields 6 cups

Christian Granger's Red Sauce

This is a unique and delicious red sauce created by Christian Granger of Crabtree, Quebec. It's highly versatile, but I like to mix it with spiral pasta, place it in a 13 X 9 casserole dish, top with a generous amount of shredded cheese (colby jack, cheddar, etc.), and bake at about 375° until the cheese is brown and bubbly. You'll need:

- 76 ounces of tomato juice
- 1 cup of ketchup
- 1 cup of Heinz chili sauce
- 1 teaspoon of parsley
- 1 teaspoon of sugar
- ½ teaspoon of cinnamon
- ½ teaspoon of ground cloves
- ½ teaspoon of marjoram
- 1 teaspoon of crushed (flakes) red pepper
- 2 bay leaves
- 1 big onion, minced
- 3 long celery sticks, minced
- 2 garlic cloves, minced
- 8 ounces of mushrooms, minced
- Tablespoon of olive oil

1) Sautee the onion, celery, mushrooms, and garlic in the olive oil until tender.
2) Simmer the remaining ingredients for 45 minutes.
3) Put all of the ingredients together and simmer for another 45 minutes.

Yields 14 cups

Yummy Guacamole

You'll need:

- 4 large or 5 medium avocados, peeled and mashed well
- 1 small red onion, chopped well
- 2 large cloves of garlic, minced
- 2 roma tomatoes, with the outer skin chopped well (no seeds)
- 1 small jalapeno pepper, diced well
- ½ cup of chopped cilantro (no stems)
- Juice of 4 limes, approximately 1/3 cup
- 1 teaspoon of salt
- 2 tablespoons of oregano

Mix all of the ingredients and refrigerate. To prevent the avocado from turning brown, pat plastic wrap down on top of the guacamole, careful not to let air in.

Kicky Cucumber Avocado Soup
(cold, great for a sore throat)

You'll need:

- 4 cups of peeled, chopped cucumbers
- 4 large (or 6 medium) peeled and pitted avocados
- ¼ cup of freshly squeezed lime juice
- 1 teaspoon of salt
- ¼ to ½ teaspoon of cayenne pepper
- ¼ cup of finely chopped cilantro, no stems
- ¼ cup of finely chopped mint leaves, no stems
- 2 cups of water

Liquefy all ingredients with a blender (regular or immersion) and keep chilled.

Yields 8 cups

Appendix B

Organizations/Websites to Learn More About Breast Cancer

- American Cancer Society (www.cancer.org);
  1-800-227-2345
  This website is for all cancers, but the breast cancer section is thorough, and if you type in any question or topic, you can usually find a good answer. The cancer glossary tool is helpful, too. Learn about cancer, treatment, research, "in the news" topics, stories of hope, support resources, and opportunities to get involved or donate. Also, this website is available in English, Spanish, Chinese, Korean, and Vietnamese.

- National Cancer Institute (www.cancer.gov);
  1-800-422-6237
  This is a very thorough site for patients and healthcare professionals on every topic

imaginable, including treatments, prevention, genetics, causes, screening and testing, statistics, clinical trials, current cancer news, cancer litera-ture, and research. It's user-friendly and avail-able in English and Spanish.

- www.breastcancer.org
  This comprehensive, user-friendly website was created by Dr. Marisa Weiss, a breast cancer oncologist. You can find information on symp-toms and diagnosis, treatment and side effects, day-to-day matters (such as paying for care, breast cancer and employment, managing med-ical records, and nutrition), lowering cancer risk, and community knowledge (discussion boards, blogs, and chat rooms). According to the website, it is "the world's most utilized online resource for medical and personal expert information on breast health and breast cancer, reaching 27 million people globally over the past 10 years."

Appendix C

Organizations/Websites that Provide Support

- Cancer Support Community (formerly Gilda's Club Worldwide and The Wellness Community) (www.cancersupportcommunity.org); 1-888-793-9355
  This organization provides support services to the friends and family members of someone diagnosed with breast cancer. As their website states, "CSC provides the highest quality emotional and social support through a network of more than 50 local affiliates, 100 satellite locations, and online."

- CANCERCare.org (www.cancercare.org); 1-800-813-4673
  CANCERcare.org provides free, professional support services to people with cancer, care-

givers, and loved ones. Programs include counseling and support groups, education, and financial assistance. Available in English and Spanish, this site also answers questions of patients, loved ones, and healthcare professionals. A list of events and opportunities to donate are offered as well.

- Cancer Treatment Centers of America (www.cancercenter.com); 1-800-615-3055 As the name suggests, this site focuses on treatment, but also offers timely, compassionate support. You can hear from survivors, find a doctor, ask questions, or receive support and guidance 24 hours a day, either on the phone or chatting live online. Email is answered within 24 hours.

Appendix D

Events/Walks
Opportunities to Volunteer or Donate
Advocacy

Most breast cancer websites have links to opportunities for all of the above. Here is a partial list:

- Susan G. Komen for the Cure (ww5.komen.org); 1-877-465-6636
  This is a comprehensive, user-friendly site with lots of information and opportunities to get involved, donate, or become an advocate for breast cancer funding and quality breast health care. Race for the Cure, the largest series of 5K runs/fitness walks in the world, raises funds and awareness while celebrating survivorship and honoring those who have lost their battle. Other Susan G. Komen events include Marathon for the Cure (running or walking a half or

full marathon), Susan G. Komen 3-Day for the Cure (60 miles in three days), and Komen on the Go (mobile education and awareness).

- American Cancer Society (www.cancer.org); 1-800-227-2345
  The American Cancer Society provides a long list of events and ways to become involved in the breast cancer community. Their Relay for Life and Making Strides Against Breast Cancer walks are well-known and incredibly uplifting. It's difficult to describe the overwhelming feeling of comradeship, but it can buoy you (whether a survivor or loved one) for weeks, maybe months. There are also many opportunities for volunteering, such as the Road to Recovery program (volunteers drive patients to and from treatment and doctors' appointments).

- Love/Avon Army of Women (www.armyofwomen.org); 1-866-569-0388 (toll free in the U.S. and Canada)
  This is an initiative of the Dr. Susan Love Research Foundation with a grant from the Avon Foundation for Women. Whether you have breast cancer or not, there are a number of studies that you can participate in "to move breast cancer beyond a cure." Working with research scientists, participants may contribute broadly, from filling out a questionnaire to being involved in clinical trials testing a new

detection marker or drug.

- Avon Walk for Breast Cancer
  (www.avonwalk.org); 1-888-540-9255
  This famous walk is held several times throughout the year in various cities across the country.
  Participants cover nearly 40 miles in two days.
  Avon's mission is to "end this deadly disease...
  the money we raise will provide women and
  men the breast cancer screening, support, and
  treatment they need regardless of their ability
  to pay, and it will help power leading-edge
  research teams across the country, fueling their
  quest for a cure."

- Pink Lotus Petals (www.pinklotuspetals.org);
  1-310-273-8002
  (affiliated with the Pink Lotus Breast Center,
  www.pinklotusbreastcenter.com)
  Pink Lotus Petals is a Los Angeles-based non-
  profit that provides free screening, diagnosis,
  surgical treatment, and post-surgical treatment
  to uninsured women and those who are unable
  to pay for care. As explained on their website,
  most breast cancer donations fund research for
  a future cure of the disease. Pink Lotus Petals,
  however, believes that saving lives now is just
  as important, and that every woman has a right
  to treatment regardless of socio-economic status
  and financial condition.

Appendix E

Movie List

We each have our own ideas about what's funny. The following list is meant to jog your memory of top comedies (critical or box office successes) from the past few decades.

Comedies from the 1970s
American Graffiti ('73)
Blazing Saddles ('74)
Young Frankenstein ('74)
Murder by Death ('76)
Oh, God! ('77)
Animal House ('78)
The In-Laws ('79)
10 ('79)

Comedies from the 1980s
Airplane ('80)

9 to 5 ('80)
Stir Crazy ('80)
History of the World, Part 1 ('81)
Stripes ('81)
Porky's ('82)
Tootsie ('82)
Trading Places ('83)
Beverly Hills Cop ('84)
Ghostbusters ('84)
Micki and Maude ('84)
Weird Science ('85)
Ruthless People ('86)
Moonstruck ('87)
Planes, Trains, and Automobiles ('87)
Raising Arizona ('87)
Three Men and a Baby ('87)
A Fish Called Wanda ('88)
Coming to America ('88)
Funny Farm ('88)
Bill & Ted's Excellent Adventure ('89)
Look Who's Talking ('89)

Comedies from the 1990s
Home Alone ('90)
What About Bob ('91)
Wayne's World ('92)
Groundhog Day ('93)
Mrs. Doubtfire ('93)
National Lampoon's Vacation ('93)
Clerks ('94)
Dumb and Dumber ('94)
The Mask ('94)

Ace Ventura When Nature Calls ('95)
Billy Madison ('95)
Mallrats ('95)
Tommy Boy ('95)
Black Sheep ('96)
The Cable Guy ('96)
Happy Gilmore ('96)
The Nutty Professor ('96)
Austin Powers ('97)
Beverly Hills Ninja ('97)
Chasing Amy ('97)
The Full Monty ('97)
Liar Liar ('97)
A Night at the Roxbury ('98)
The Big Lebowski ('98)
Rushmore ('98)
There's Something About Mary ('98)
The Waterboy ('98)
The Wedding Singer ('98)
American Pie ('99)
Big Daddy ('99)
Bowfinger ('99)
Office Space ('99)

Comedies from 2000 on

Bedazzled ('00)
Big Momma's House ('00)
Meet the Parents ('00)
Me, Myself, and Irene ('00)
Scary Movie ('00)
Legally Blond ('01)
Shallow Hal ('01)

My Big Fat Greek Wedding ('02)
Anger Management ('03)
Bad Santa ('03)
Bringing Down the House ('03)
Bruce Almighty ('03)
Old School ('03)
Mean Girls ('04)
Napoleon Dynamite ('04)
Are We There Yet? ('05)
The 40-Year Old Virgin ('05)
Wedding Crashers ('05)
Borat ('06)
Night at the Museum ('06)
Knocked Up ('07)
Norbit (2007)
Pineapple Express ('08)
Step Brothers ('08)
Extract ('09)
Ghosts of Girlfriends Past ('09)
The Hangover ('09)
The Invention of Lying ('09)
The Proposal ('09)
Zombieland ('09)
Cop Out ('10)
Date Night('10)
Due Date ('10)
Dinner for Schmucks ('10)
Get Him to the Greek ('10)
Grown Ups ('10)
Hot Tub Time Machine ('10)
Jackass 3D ('10)
Little Fockers ('10)

Movie List

The Other Guys ('10)
Scott Pilgrim vs. the World ('10)
Bad Teacher ('11)
Big Mommas: Like Father, Like Son ('11)
Bridesmaids ('11)
Crazy, Stupid, Love ('11)
Hall Pass ('11)
The Hangover Part 2 ('11)
Horrible Bosses ('11)
Just Go With It ('11)
Madea's Big Happy Family ('11)
Paul ('11)
What's Your Number? ('11)
Zookeeper ('11)

Endnotes

The Purpose of This Book
1. American Cancer Society, "What are the key statistics about breast cancer?" http://www.cancer.org/Cancer/BreastCancer/DetailedGuide/breast-cancer-key-statistics, March 6, 2011.
2. American Cancer Society, "What are the key statistics about breast cancer in men?" www.cancer.org/Cancer/BreastCancerinMen/DetailedGuide/breast-cancer-in-men-key-statistics, October 18, 2011.

Chapter 1
3. Elisabeth Kubler-Ross, On Death & Dying (New York: Macmillan, 1969), 51-123.
4. Susan M. Love, M.D., with Karen Lindsey, Dr. Susan Love's Breast Book (Philadelphia, PA: Da Capo Press, 2010), 102-107.

5. American Cancer Society, "How is Breast Cancer Diagnosed?" http://www.cancer.org/docroot/CRI 2 4 3X How is breast cancer diagnosed, August 13, 2009

6. American Cancer Society, "Imaging-Guided Breast Biopsy," http:www.cancer.org/Treatment/UnderstandingYour Diagnosis/ExamsandTestDescription, February 20, 2011.

7. Ibid.

8. American Cancer Society, "Some with Breast Cancer May Be Able to Skip Full Node Removal," http://www.cancer.org/Cancer/news/News/some-with-breast-cancer-may-be-able-to-skip-full-lymph-node-removal, February 9, 2011.

9. Love, 295.

10. Ibid.

11. "Understanding Breast Cancer: Reading Your Pathology Report," Sanofi-Aventis, US.DOC.0.06.112, July, 2007, page 4.12.

http://www.cancer.org/docroot/CRI 2 4 3X How is breast cancer diagnosed.

13. American Cancer Society, "How is Breast Cancer Staged?" http://www.cancer.org/docroot/CRI/content/CRI 2 4 3X How is breast cancer staged, August 13, 2009.

14. Ibid.

15. Ibid.

16. Ibid.

17. Dr. Bruce A. Feinberg, Understanding and Fighting

Breast Cancer: Breast Cancer Answers (Decatur, GA: Lenz Books, 2009), pp. 31-33.

18. Agendia.com, "Mammaprint®/Genomic Testing for Breast Cancer Prognosis and Treatment," http://www.agendia.com/pages/home/1.php, February 22, 2011.

19. Web MD, "Oncotype DX Test for Breast Cancer," http://www.webmd.com/breast-cancer/oncotype-dx-test-breast-cancer?page=2, October 16, 2011.

20. Sanofi-Aventis, pp. 7-10; Dr. Kristi Funk, October, 2011.

Chapter 2

21. Love, 456.

22. Ibid., pp. 366-367.

23. American Cancer Society, "Radiation Therapy," http://www.cancer.org/docroot/CRI/content/CRI_2_4_4X_Radiation_Therapy_5.asp?rnav, August 13, 2009.

24. American Cancer Society, "Targeted Therapy," http://www.cancer.org/docroot/CRI/content/CRI_2_4_4X_Targeted_Therapy_5.asp?rnav=cri, August 13, 2009.

Chapter 3

25. Love, 541.

26. Feinberg, 68.

27. "Understanding Breast Cancer and Treatment Options: A Guidebook for Patients and Caregivers," AstraZeneca Pharmaceuticals, 2008, page 31.

28.

http://www.cancer.org/docroot/CRI/content/CRI_2_4_4X_Targeted_Therapy_5.asp?rnav=cri

Chapter 4

29. Laura Pensiero, R.D., Susan Oliveria, ScD., M.P.H., with Michael Osborne, M.D., The Strang Cookbook for Cancer Prevention (New York, NY: Dutton, 1998), 3.

30. National Cancer Institute, "Antioxidants and Cancer Prevention," http://www.cancer.gov/cancertopics/factsheet/prevention/antioxidants, March 6, 2011.

31. Pensiero, 12.

32. Ibid.

33. American Cancer Society, "Phytochemicals," http://www.cancer.org/Treatment/TreatmentandSideEffects/ComplementaryandAlternativeMedicine/HerbsVitaminsandMinerals/phytochemicals, March 6, 2011.

34. Ibid.

35. Ibid.

36. Kimberly Mathai, MS, RD, with Ginny Smith, The Cancer Lifeline Cookbook (Seattle, WA: Sasquatch Books, 2004), 3.

37. LiveStrong.com, "Top Cancer Fighting Foods," http://www.livestrong.com/article/993394-top-cancerfighting-foods/, March 5, 2011.

38. Ibid.

39. Mathai, 2.

40. Pensiero, 12.

41. American Institute for Cancer Research, "Foods That Fight Cancer?"

http://www.aicr.org/site/PageServer?pagename=food
sthatfightcancer, March 5, 2011.
42.
http://www.aicr.org/site/PageServer?pagename=food
sthatfightcancer
43. LiveStrong.com, "Top Ten Cancer-Fighting Foods,"
http://www.livestrong.com/article/85939-top-ten-
cancerfighting-foods/, March 5, 2011.
44. Hope Ricciotti, M.D., and Vincent Connelly, The
Breast Cancer Prevention Cookbook (New York, NY:
W.W. Norton & Company, Inc., 2002), 15.
45. Mathai, 7.
46.
http://www.aicr.org/site/PageServer?pagename=food
sthatfightcancer
47. Ibid.
48.
http://www.aicr.org/site/PageServer?pagename=food
sthatfightcancer
49. Mathai, 12.
50. http://www.livestrong.com/article/85939-top-ten-
cancerfighting-foods/
51. Mathai, 9.
52. Ibid.
53.
http://www.aicr.org/site/PageServer?pagename=food
sthatfightcancer
54. Mathai, 6.
55. Ibid.
56.

http://www.aicr.org/site/PageServer?pagename=food
sthatfightcancer

57. LiveStrong.com, "Cancer Super Foods,"
http://www.livestrong.com/article/269998-cancer-
super-foods/, March 5, 2011

58. Ricciotti, 17.

59. Pensiero, 13.

60. Mathai, 11.

61. Elaine Magee, M.P.H., R.D., Tell Me What to Eat to
Help Prevent Breast Cancer (New York, NY: Rosen
Publishing Group, Inc., 2002), 29.

62.
http://www.aicr.org/site/PageServer?pagename=food
sthatfightcancer

63.
http://www.aicr.org/site/PageServer?pagename=food
sthatfightcancer

64. Magee, 28

65. Magee, 32.

66. Mathai, 8.

67. Ibid.

68.
http://www.aicr.org/site/PageServer?pagename=food
sthatfightcancer

69. Preventdisease.com, "Could Guacamole be the
Ultimate Cancer Fighting Food?"
http://preventdisease.com/news/10/080410_guacomo
le_cancer.shtml, March 13, 2011.

70. Calavo.com, "Avocado Nutrition,"
http://www.calavo.com/nutrition.php, March 13,

2011.

Final Thoughts
71.
http://www.cancer.org/Cancer/BreastCancer/Detaile dGuide/breast-cancer-key-statistics, March 6, 2011.

Cover designed by Doug Quinn

Made in the USA
Charleston, SC
17 October 2012